The People`s Army`s Revolution!

*The **battleplan against** the **NWO**!*

By Thomas Eidsaa last edited 13.04.2020

A compilation of articles, read alongside internet.

Exposing and defeating the black magic NWO!

I wish you a happy revolution! *Be careful!* We are not fighting an armed conflict but an infowar. ¨Peace love anarchy!¨

PS! My Christian book series are national-conservative and religious conservative. This book is more liberal, ***dedicated*** to **why** we **need a revolution** and the few ways of **actually achieving revolution**.

Cover and all writing by Thomas Eidsaa copyright 2019.

Other books by Thomas Eidsaa:

The GRRRRR book-series, or The Great Romantic Revivalist`s Reformation Revolution Renaissance series, is a an eye-opening Christian series which detail all my research into Christianity, neo-charismatic theology, apologetics, ontological arguments, the problem of evil, eschatology, and conspiracy theories of great importance every Christian needs to understand.

It is a work aimed at waking you up and expose the evil you never thought existed.
What you don`t know can still kill you.
It is a guide, and compendium of important topics relating to the radical, Christian faith in the dangerous, unpredictable 21st century death of Europe.

I take the reader on an amazing journey – uniting 1st century Nazarene knowledge with 21st century science, theology and societal problems. I personally believe the knowledge therein will create peace on Earth.

I believe Christians hold sole responsibility for the Earth and must act as such.
I have therefore created the Ontological, Metaphysical Law of Source, Love and Light. which I hope will be the universal, humanistic, inter-religious scientific religion, and bedrock of a future Golden Age Utopia, upon which all differences are set aside.
I also believe the neo-charismatic, Pentecostal Christians deserve their own nation by now, being the largest growing Christian group, which I dedicated myself to see happen as outlined in the Kingdom of God, where I outline a utopian system of Christian governance that I hope can be a light for all nations...

Books in the GRRRRR series.

1. The God Reality? Scientific proof of ¨God¨? And the scientific religion of Source, Love and Light.
2. The Secrets of St. John`s Revelations – The Revelation Conspiracies!
3. Jesus, Lucifer and the ritual of the cross explained – How Jesus was the messiah.
4. The Wisdom of All Golden Ages – The ontological, metaphysical law of source, love and light!
5. The Christian Path – Biblical Theology – The Last Reformation! (This book has no conspiracy, or controversial topics, and relates to every Pentecostal and Neo-Charismatic Christian.
6. The Kingdom of God – Strategies to guarantee global Christian utopia!

Other books:

- The People`s Army`s Red Revolution – A revolutionary`s handbook!
- How to make the world`s best Orgonite – All mistakes so you don`t have to.
- A Christian Martyr in Kristiansand – The diary of the Turin-Shroud God experiment.

Conspiracy realities to study.

*How can you explain to your children that you lived, knew of the evil,
yet didn`t lead the parade against the evil of this age? Once you
open your eyes to heresy and conspiracy, how can close them
without a guilty conscience before God?*
*What your teachers, government and media tell you isn`t true and
you know it! You`ve been living inside a dream-world since you were
born!*
I will teach you revolution.
*We face censorship, and a much greater threat: Communist police-
states.*

This book is a compilation of many articles I wrote over the years
2017-19, and assumes the reader has a knowledge-basis within
several conspiracy-theory topics, most prominently:

The financial tyranny (of f.i the Rothschild banking dynasty) , the
food and water poisoning, aerosol AI smartdust from planes called
"chemtrails" infecting all humans with AI self-replicating Morgellon
fibers, the dangers of 5g, the AI possessed skynet "cybersatan"
mark of the beast cpu Matrix simulation/surveillance of all life, to
overwrite our reality to control every human on the planet, the
Rockefeller Cardigan FDA conspiracy, the conspiracy to hush down
major medical breakthroughs e.g cancer cures, the Sabbatean
Frankist Thelema antichrist religion of the elite, the Jesuit-
Sabbatean-Illuminati-Satanic interconnection since the 16th-18th
century up until today, and their conspiracy (organized anti-human-
activists whose religion is destruction/everything inverted) of the
abovementioned who infiltrated all religions and all sectors of
society with their inhuman poison, exposing proofs of this
conspiracy: Jewish and religious elite who are Satanic/Sabbatean
Frankists (Vatican, Bohemian Club, OTO, Satanism etc), the
educational conspiracy to construct a false theory of physics,
evolution, math, and all other scholarly fields (check out David
Wilcock`s Wisdom Teachings, Wilhelm Reich and Michael Tellinger)
, the Reptilian shapeshifter conspiracy (check out David Icke and
interdimensional physics) , the giant human skeletal remains cover-

up (again check out Michael Tellinger), extinct human dwarves, giants, (Sylvie Ivanova www.megaliths.org newearth youtube channel) hybrids, "alien species", etc, the Nazi relocation to Antarctica (Jim Wilhelmson's Beyond Science Fiction) and Vimanna/UFO technology, the conspiracy to destroy nation, race, culture, and identity disguised as "eliminating polarities in the name of freedom and equality", and the plans to rule guised as spacemen, the so called "false flag alien invasion", false flag terror attacks in general, the Federal Reserve system, debt based economy, the Rothschild Sabbatean Illuminati banking-elite, and how they created and financed all revolutions and wars of the last 300 years including the French revolution, and the Bolshevik revolution, the depopulation agenda 21 (check out David Icke) and the NWO plans for a worldwide communist dictatorship, etc... And lots more. But if you could check yes on this list, then this is the book for you. As a former Jew, I was appalled when I learnt of Sabbatai Zevi and Jacob Frank's antichrist inversion of Judaism and their effect on the Illuminati. I puked, cried, and was disgusted by the thought of calling myself an Israelite or "human" for that matter. The Sabbatean-Frankist-Illuminati conglomerate conspiracy is a matter of fact, and the root conspiracy beneath all others. The founder of the Church of Satan, Anton LaVey (Levi by birthname) was also a Jew. Their sadomasochistic sodomy anal and pedophilia perversion and rituals of murder must be exposed at all costs. Sinning was somewhat innocent until the antichrist, Sabbatai Zevi came along and got over 1000.000 Jewish followers proclaiming he was the Messiah in 1666. Do your research on YouTube, Wikipedia, etc. We will use terms like "Jewish-masonic" and "Satanic Illuminati" as they are infiltrated by Sabbateanism. Here's mankind's battleplan:

Reed out the corrupt career politicians, the financial elite cause of wars, and the technocratic elite. Let investigative journalism media disclose REAL truth, history, science, and medical technology, dealing with these THREE elites first, enlightening the west, and WATCH as the humanistic west peacefully returns to harmony automatically, integrating Muslims into an intellectual humanistic society 100% naturally.

Reed out the cause of the problem, and the problem will die of naturally. And the problem is certainly not immigrants. We are way beyond that and face much graver fortunes. The cause of the problem of immigration is the trade-federation conglomerate, (their business empire) and their WAR.

Reed out the Satanic cause, and THEN handle its problems: Wars, poor immigrants, and fascist RELIGION, all sponsored by multinational conglomerates in the Jewmerican Union popularly called the ¨New World (dis)Order, which the People`s Army must overtake.

That was my intro. Now I will show you how EASY it is to get back your freedom!

Table of content:

Chapter 1: Why we must fight!

Let`s get right to it! I mentioned quite a few conspiracies above, so why not take you through the largest and most secret? The ones you need to understand. Let`s begin with an alternative history lesson based on the research of Russian mathematician and new history chronologist, Dr. Anatoly Fomenko! I can only give you the clues, you have to read his books and watch his videos yourself.

HISTORY IS WRONG! Research alternative chronology by Anatoly Fomenko and the material of Sylvie Ivanova.

Have you ever heard of the mud-flood of the 19th century? What if I told you that the controllers of domed Earth who created all religions have reset civilization several times in the last 1000 years, and that we are approaching a new reset when the blonde race will even be forgotten from history? There is proof to show it. What if the book of Revelations could be dated to the 16th century, by Anatoly Fomenko, and is a work to frame Christianity and make Jesus the antichrist 666? There is proof to show it – the length Satan would go to undo the character, work, and memory of Jesus, even resetting civilization in the 18th century mudflood for the completion of his antichrist plan.

Now don`t get me wrong. I`m not your regular mud-flooder, and it`s not really about mud: *It`s more about the technology and civilizations the mud destroyed,* something Sylvie Ivanova has a YouTube channel called ¨newearth¨ about, having made the best 26 episode long documentary on mankind`s TRUE history available anywhere on the planet, based on Russian mathematician Anatoly Fomenko`s 22 books on New Chronology and her own extensive research at her website, www.megaliths.org Here is the 26 episode documentary I finished watching yesterday.
https://www.youtube.com/watch?v=bk-o42NNQm4&list=PLJk0yT4erxuRcCMBujshjWZ-KNAHAWCx6&index=1

Here is my playlist for all other important topics concerning this age:

https://www.youtube.com/playlist?list=PLIwCcxviHTNkCJE-JGm5lUym11ngjBxqxc

This is top secret stuff they don`t want you to know about!

But before you embark on the greatest of all conspiracies, I recommend researching at the only alternative history forum, www.stolenhistory.org , including the mysterious mudflood/mud-rain topic of regular resets of humanity by the controllers of this Matrix. At the forum, you will find great posts about Tartary, the 1000 invented years, and the ¨pious fraud¨ of the Catholic monks who re-wrote history alongside Joseph Scalliger to start a New World Order illegitimately based on the Judeo-Christian Greek-Roman invented civilization. I also compiled the best (as of today) mud-flood, reset, and alternative history videos in this playlist, many of which are second range productions, while others are scholarly and factually based. https://www.youtube.com/playlist?list=PLIwCcxvi-HTNmyQL6cpHLxz6ktEowxlFCa

Alternative history, resets by the controller (Elohim), and massive geo-engineering by them, as in the mudflood, are an upcoming branch of what would easily be seen as fringe, even by conspiracy-reality related groups and people. But put all your beliefs on the shelf for a week and re-evaluate your reality afterwards.

The work of Anatoly Fomenko is supported by the top world Chess player, Russian Gary Kasparov and many others.

Real history, not that which is taught by quackademics, point to our western civilization as Slavic and/or ¨Nordic/Caucasian/Aryan¨ in origin, with a ¨Roman-medieval¨ cover up. The greatest conspiracy is that of covering up the world`s true history.

These Slavs, blondes, redhead, and races extinct, came as a remnant and called themselves the ¨scattered ones/the Russia¨ as translated from Slavic. Their ¨Roman¨ architecture, most of which is in Turkey, and from North America to China, not in Rome, is proof of a global coherent culture whose controlled downfall 200 years ago, was necessary for the rise of quackademia. Scalar weapons, giants, atmospheric "Tesla" electricity already 400 years ago, megalithic building techniques and true sciences based on alchemy and the ETHER were part of the reasons why the controllers, the syndicate trade-federation, called "the New Atlantis", profited from the downfall of this first worldwide Empire of Great Tartary (TartARYA), where the Caucasian Khans of Tartary ruled. (There never was a mongol Empire, the Great Khan trans. Genghis Khan was a blonde or red-head Tartarian, depending on sources.)

Blonde and redhead mummies, depictions, with coherent burial and daily life culture are found from south-America to China, the "un-readable" Etruscan (early "Roman") alphabet is readable by any Slavic-speaking person, the mameluke Egyptians were blonde Slavs, Genghis Khan was the blonde or redheaded Emperor of Tar-tary, (who was not a Mongol), Napoleon fought Tartary along with the Romanovs, discrediting history as proven by coins, blondes ap-pear in North America, South America, New-Zealand, and the Ber-ber/Barbar tribe of north Africa still hold onto their Slavic culture of cloths, prior to any colonization, the New World Order beginning with the Phoenician Jews, continuing through Rome, through Eu-rope, and was already planned out and finalized as the world today; already by the invention of the heliocentric model and the coloniza-tion era, (E.g Cortes the Spanish Conquistador general and his massacre) a collaboration of all Christian Europe to destroy all Ar-yan survivors, the Tartarian empire, the African cultures, the Asian cultures, with massacres.

These "Russia/scattered ones" whom civilized the world after a very real catastrophe about 7000 years ago, giving rise to the Jew-ish/Phoenician and Russian calendar, popularly called the fall of At-lantis, which was actually not an Island, but a civilization that fell, was needless to say the enemy of the NWO political narrative of cul-tural-Marxism and globalism. After endless, peaceful domination by the blonde Tartars, the western Satanists of Christianity destroyed the entire world at the time of a great natural catastrophe known as the "mudflood", using it as a reset of civilization, burying our history, introducing new people, and a new model of science and history: Great Tartary: The Greatest cover-up of all time.

Anatoly Fomenko also proves that when Joseph Scaliger, a chronologist, rewrote history for the pope, and purposefully invented 1000 years, converting the "i" for "Iesus" to a "1", so that the dates of ancient coins where it says i656 would by historians today be read as 1656. This was purposeful for the pope and Scaliger, a French Jesuit whose father was named Julius Caesar, as they both invented new calendars. Scaliger invented the Julian calendar, named after his father. The Gregorian calendar of BC (before Christ) and A.D (anno domine/In the year of our Lord) was declared the new worldwide calendar by pope Gregory 13th in 1582.

You might think the war on whites is a new phenomenon? TPTB have worked hard for our true blonde history to be forgotten, considering the blonde aboriginal New-Zealanders, many blonde Aztecs, the African blonde Berber tribe of the former country of Barbaria, the blonde Genghis Khan and the Golden Hoarde of Tartary (known by their golden hair), the Goths, the caucasian Chineese, and the Mameluke dynasty of Egypt before Napoleon being BLONDE CAUCASIANS, according to the real history presented by Fomenko and Ivanova, Genghis meaning only "great", as any of the emperors of Great Tartary, with the story about Mongolian horseriders completely invented, Mongolia having only 20.000 citizens only 100 years ago, who knew nothing of a Genghis Khan.

It was in fact the blonde-redhaired Slavic people from the river Volga, who dominated all world history and created all civilization, including the Vedic, the Christian, the Egyptian and the South America civilizations, all based from Great Tartary. The so-called unreadable ancient early-Roman Etruscan alphabet in Jerusalem and everywhere else, at the time of Jesus, can be read by any Slavic person today, as both the Greeks, and Etruscan/early Romans, etc, were caucasian Slavs, dominated by the Eastern Empires of that time.

Anatoly Fomenko proves with mathematics that the Biblical and historical Kingdoms of the dark ages – ancient times, were invented. He proved this by math, mapping what he called "phantom dynasties", dynasties made up for us to believe our civilization is Judeo-Roman and not Slavic, giving power to the Satanic European "New Atlantis trade federation" / the New World Order planned with the Phoenician invention of Abrahamic literature, enforced since the 15/500's, which ended in the carpet bombing and mud-flooding of Great Tartary, the last stronghold of humanity, an empire bigger than Russia once.

Google Anatoly Fomenko's works, "New Chronology phantom dynasties", and see with 1000000-1 absolute proof, that the Kings, stories and Kingdoms of Judah and Israel never existed, the new and old testament being only fictional, with Slavic language found all over Jerusalem, and the Mediterranean, everywhere, and with the *ancient* Roman empire, nor Greek culture ever existing (in the form we learn today), Rome emerging in the late middle ages, as there never was a Jesus, Pilate, a Herod, or a temple of Solomon. Further proof that the Greek-Roman and Hebrew language and history was invented by a supercomputer/the writing of the Bible after a reset, comes with the unexplainable 7-digit numeric code of gematria found throughout the entire new and old testament, as discovered by Ivan Panin.

How can this be true? How could the peasant class not notice they added 1000 years by gradually making the i into a 1? Look at late medieval coins and dates. Look at maps. The mudflood alternative history is not a hypothesis, it's an irrefutable scientific fact. Most great cities in the world, from Russia to Paris to England to America were buried in up to 25 meters of mud (in the case of "the hole in Paris"), but we don't know how. Some theorize there were several mudfloods, one also in the 1600's, and that the controllers are fallen angels based in higher dimensions, in Antarctica and underground bases, capable of Matrix reality control beyond our imaginations, who fooled us with the Bible, and plagiarized the Slavic Pharaoh Osiris Jesus into Greek-Roman version of history.

Angkor Wat, the ruins of Egypt, and most ruins of the pre-flood world of Tartary were shining until 200+ years ago, and Columbus never discovered America, where early maps and explorer diaries tell of marvellous Roman-style cities, with aqueducts standing til this day. Napoleon destroyed the blonde Mameluke dynasty of Christian Egypt, vandalizing all ruins, sending the back into ancient times when they were shining only 250 years ago… He ordered his men to shoot the sphinx, there are countless sources. Pagan Egypt never existed and the hieroglyphs told stories of the Bible, before a false Egyptian alphabet was introduced after much effort.

We`re talking of an age of elites, where the west were basically slaves to the great Russian hoard, known as the ¨golden hoard¨, as all describe their horsemen as blonde. Through allying with the fallen angels, the west won the war and destroyed all high-culture, all true science and the white race, the blonde Slavs, the chosen people of the Sun, who Jesus was off.

But how??? Benedictine monks rewrote history in the (i100-i200) 11th-12th century, plagiarizing Osiris Jesus, and the Vatican Jesuits continued to rewrite history in regular resets, by copying ancient texts into something completely new, with the original texts always conveniently lost in church-fires. Today, we have not a single reliable text older than 400-500 years, and although these texts claim they`re copies of older texts, all texts admit to ¨adopting history to the most recent opinion,¨ the Pope`s opinion. Supposedly the only ancient texts we have, like the Nag Hammadi and Dead-Sea scrolls, etc, are certainly fake. There are no old Bibles or old Qurans in the world, both having been re-written many times. There is no cemetery older than 200 years anywhere in the world, only Jewish ones, as the reset destroyed all traces of the old i/iesus calendar system, adding 1000 years to history. We advanced technology and electricity, tanks, helicopters, airplanes and nuclear bombs at the time of the Napoleon wars.

Jesus was a composite figure, or the true name of the true God of the survivors/Slavs, from what we know. Jesus might very well be God himself, while the invented history of Abrahamism being pagan.

The purpose of inverting, perverting, and destroying history, cosmology and science with replacement of false ones, adding 1000 artificial years to our calendar, as done by the Jesuits, Benedictine monks, and Joseph Scallinger, is seen today, deceiving humanity to think that peaceful, global high-tech civilizations never existed, and that there has always been war. But reality is that mankind prospered and built Tartarian ("Roman") megalithic structures from Japan to North and South America (prior to Columbus) , which we cannot replicate today, with "Tesla" etheric/atmospheric electricity only 250 years ago...

And if any of these peaceful Eastern civilizations, vassal-states of the Tartarian Empire, like the Khmer Dynasty that made Angkor Wat ever wanted world domination, we would be speaking their language now, but the Phoenicians/Jews, with their occult sorcery, conquered the world through black magick. Look at the level of technology and the giant doors, giant books, and giant skeletal remains all over the world. IF the giants of Tartary would have wanted world domination, they certainly would have succeeded.

Do you really believe it`s natural human behaviour to war other nations regularly every 30-40 years, as false European history and false Bible stories tells us? 1000.000 Ethiopians dying in Israel? Solomon having 1000 wives? The Talmud telling of how Rome killed 16 million Jewish infants? These fabrications of war, fabrications of false science, and all others, are to make us dependent on the state for protection, materialistic, predatorial and individualistic: Caught in an everlasting illusion. "Survival of the fittest."

Fomenko: Revelations is the NWO battleplan written by the devil in the 16-17th century?

Jesus Mazzaroth astrological birth-tale of the gospels coincides with the astrology of Revelations, (a book which Anatoly Fomenko proved was created by monks in the 16-17th century, as Rev. 12 has Jesus astrological birthdate, 19.08.01 BC, proven by Mazzaroth astrology as discovered by Alan Tat, sending Jesus back over 1000 years before he ever existed, proving that the gospels (story about Christ`s birth) were ALSO edited at the time of the creation of Revelations, discrediting the entire Bible EVEN more, as the story of Christ had to coincide with Joseph Scalliger`s false history chronology, sending Christ 1000 years back in time.

Revelations is a book for population control, to incite fear and incite Satanism, their plan of a one-world monetary New World Order, their religion of the dragon whore and beast, the idea of ¨eating the whore¨, and to prepare for their version of Jesus 2nd coming, where Jesus chi xi stigma 666 is the beast, God of the old testament (Rev. 13:16 vs Exodus 13:1) (a time which time never existed). Got that? Read it again.

Revelations is a book created to undo Christ`s 1st coming, create the false Jesus, create a Satanic cult, and create a Satanic 2nd coming as an evil betting game. Creating fear, wars, natural disasters, (e.g the seven bowls, seals and trumpets) , all under authority by the Pope (God) and by the billions of Christians who believe Revelations to be authentic.

The entire idea of creating Christianity, the myth of ANCIENT Israel (which never existed, Phoenicia did however exist), Judaism and Islam, around the (i100) 11th century, the 1st century after Christ, separating previously united religions, *was to unify the west against what history wrongly assumes as the East-Roman Empire, a part of the Slavic Tartarian Empire*, which in reality existed prior to Rome, and dominated all the known world. The West wanted to free themselves from eternal domination of what was known as Tartary, the (blonde) golden horde as they were called. Through 1000 years of Jewish/Phoenician black magic, lies, and all forms of population control, the extra-terrestrial helped the west to destroy human civilization forever, 200 years ago, introducing the New World Order and the false Jesus, the invented Jesus of the invented Revelations of the invented Abrahamism, defaming and killing the noble giants, the angelic Slavs, and their great horde of Tartary, 7000 years of peaceful megalithic civilization, buried under mud.

Jesus the Slavic-Egyptian messiah of the Turkish pre-Roman empire messed around somewhere, perhaps in Judea, about 1000 years ago, while some sources, like ¨The Travels of Noah into Europe¨ dated i600 something, tells Jesus existed about 3000 years ago. Jesus was also Osiris, and a pagan Egypt never existed. They made up the gospels, the history, and what of the 7 digit system of the Bible…? Read Fomenko. Was the New and Old testament written in the (i.100) 11th century at the same time, probably about a fictional character??? Anatoly believes so!
But if Jesus was entirely fictional, how did they get away with it? Ergo, Jesus must either have been/is the true creator God, in whatever form, and/or there was a civilization reset inducting our ancestors with the obviously made up story about Jesus.
But you might say: If it wasn`t a staged coup, as it seems with the 7 digit pattern, how did the entire world start recording dates after Christ? How did Christianity explode globally, even to Europe in 100 years, if it wasn`t just made up? First of all, we don`t know that, and secondly, most of the Earth used the calendar of the survivors, the calendar the Jews adopted, the true Slavic calendar still used by some in Russia, which was 6000 years old at that time. But most probably: The story of Jesus was built on a historical person, and/or the mythology of the true creator, making the Bible utterly false, but true in it`s mystery teachings and wisdom: Cause who creates a sacred 7-digit coded book anyways?

Ok. So history and religion is a tool of population control. But that was just the beginning!

Why we must fight - the ultimate mark of the beast!

I deserve my rights but have none! The Norwegian police-state should be considered an illegal force of violent population control, but have authorized gangstalking, and electronic harassment on unknowing citizens, as they test out the mark-of-the-beast on me unwillingly like a lab-rat for no other reason than them being technocrat madscientists, antihuman misanthropist activist, antichrist activists, and population control extremists, testing out the mark-of-the-beast system on an upright, kind, beautiful, talented, loving and naïve innocent civilian psychiatric patient, as so many before me. Our community of millions beast-targeted Christians (the targeted individuals community) suffer the same symptoms and mostly all of us are Christian. The secret intelligence agencies have long experimented mixing technology and black magick for population control experimentation, as black magicians were the first intelligence agencies, the art of creating change and maniupulation from a distance, which we read off in the Bible. The PST (Norway`s Politiets Sikkerhets Tjeneste) , and much of corporate Norway (if not all) are part of this ¨Crowleyan, Thelemic Antichrist *Activist*¨ NWO and mark-of-the-beast *transhumanist agenda*, which I will explain to you what is.

Your body works because of nerves and neurons that transmit electrical signals. Scientists have been able to create robot prosthetics for amputees. The secret military science are even further down the road, with CIA`s Mk-Ultra project battling Russia for having the best mind-control technology to affect hostile individuals, groups and nations during the dangerous, unpredictable cold war. Even the Nazis were deep into mind-control. The technology exists today, but the question is: Will it be abused? Power and madscientists ultimate dream, controlling minds, acting on the prophesies of St.John WILL be abused and I am a victim of it. Will it be commercialized? Elon Musk has stated that humans need mind to computer and computer to mind interface technology to keep up with the technological evolution. This will be the next technological step in commercial products, marketed as ¨the coolest technological innovation of all time!¨ And it could be, depending on if you use it or misuse it.

We already have robot lenses, implantable microchips, and are dependent on wearable electronic gadgets to operate, like the Iphone. Siri and Alexa (of google), the AI assistants of today, process all words spoken from all humans, all movements by all humans, all info about all humans, and all internet traffic by all humans to create a profile. This is why if you visit, a tea-store, or talk about babies you will see tea adds or baby adds on facebook and YouTube recommendations etc. The government, controlled by an AI computer that is the incarnation/possessed of Satan, governs all human affairs, video-calls, bank-transfer, and knows everything about every human on Earth. The government knows everything about you. Is this not a totalitarian state? Totalitarian in what way? In that it is ruled by technocrats/madscientists, and black-military underground projects: All who are antichrist activists and wants the superpowers of technology, robotics, cybernetics, neuronic implants (brain implants), that will be on the market soon. Every kid would want the latest and best technology, the excitement of entering virtual realities, or the ability to control his computer only by his thoughts.

This has been prophesied about and has been the ultimate dream of Satan since the beginning. But can the technology become self aware? Can the technology control you? Is this Satan`s way to artificially bind every Christian to demonic entities through possessive technology that controls you instead of you controlling it??? This is what me and millions of other targeted individuals testify. That a computer (Siri or Alexa, which is basically the same computer, Satan Himself) with our profile, reads our minds and directs our chain of thought, speech and acts to possess us with spirits. It is the ultimate form of torture and oppression: Fighting an infinitely high IQ computer from taking over your mind.

What are chemtrails and Morgellons? Chemtrails vs contrails.

A contrail (condensated hot air from the plane-engine) will always dissipate, even at high altitudes, that is a scientific fact, while chemtrails are those 5 planes you saw spraying the sky until all blue was gone from the trail-expansion, bright metal-particles blotting out the sun creating a whitish silvery haze.

Chemtrails are an airplane-sprayed deadly tonic of nano-particles, particularly aluminium, barium and strontium with an ENORMOUS surface area, a mere ounce being able to cover a square kilometre in a thick silvery haze, talking pyrotechnic experience here. Chemtrails officially doesn`t exist, but is the largest black-market industry of today, and undisputedly exists. It serves many purposes, developed by America, a patented and real technology from the madscientists of the cold war. One such purpose is in conjunction with the HAARP facilities program`s electromagnetic and etheric radiation of the chemtrail created clouds, as the aluminium absorbs the ions of HAARP beamed electricity, enabling weather control e.g high pressure and low pressure, etc, and they`ve become really good at it. The chemtrails can be charged so it will or won`t create natural clouds, depending, as I am sure you have seen.
The chemtrails also serve another purpose, mind control, as they may contain, depending on time and place; black-goo, viruses, fungal-spores, that sweet chlorine-peaches scent (the poison scent) synonymous with silvery spraying days, most easily smelled in warmer weather, a sweet scent you might associate with warm summer days, perfuming the chemtrails, a scent you even might want to fill your lungs with, or at least, that`s the perfume`s purpose, because the most dangerous component in chemtrails is aimed at the lungs of the population; self-replicating nano-particle polymer fibers (Morgellons). Chemtrails is the most closely guarded and most important aspect of the New World Order, for purposes of weather-control (catastrophes, draughts, etc) and mind control (through Morgellons).

Morgellons can also grow LARGE polymer fibres in itchy clusters under your skin. I only had 3-4 such clusters, but eliminated them with Oregano oil and Borax, the only ailments to prevent them from spreading further.

Google: Self-replicating Morgellons polymer fibres drawn from the skin of a victim. Notice the bright red and blue colours. Is this something you want growing inside you, connected to a chip, and taking you over? The internet floods over with such images. Morgellons disease was planned not to develop, and is an unwanted overgrowth by the polymer fibres whose real purpose I will explain below.

What is going on? Satan`s mark 666 masterplan exposed!

The Christian targeted individuals' community (test subjects) all have the same symptoms: Whenever we start a thought, the computer mind-thought in our head takes over and turns it into something sinful, wrong or bad, based on the script. The technology then transfers accusative demons to possess you, voodoo stab you, etc, artificially based upon you unwillingly following the induced mind-controlled script of these sinful thoughts (which you had no control over) , thus artificially draining soul, e.g artificially opening up an astral gate/giving the black magic entry into your soul to control you. Completely computerized by Satan, who IS the computer. Why does he target mostly Christians, but also non-conformative intelligent people, and conspiracy-realist scientists?

From millions of attacked Christian testimonies, we can thus conclude that 1 not only is Siri/Alexa/Skynet (like in the Terminator movies) Satan himself (the world supercomputer IS Satan Himself reincarnate), 2 he has an electric grid inside our brains connecting all our neurons to a GPS capable micro-computer that transfers all YOUR thoughts to the ¨world-computer which we call ¨Cybersatan`s¨ ID profile of YOU through the internet ** and/or by military drones (evil UFO`s) depending on your location *, 3 AND also (the brain-chip-computer) acts as a *receiver* for Satan/Cybersatan`s response/answer to your thoughts through the *ethernet*, and (the computer/microchip) further transmits this to your neurons/brain with lightening speed, so: 1 From brain to chip, 2 from chip to Sky, 3 demonic calculation in Sky, 4 transmission back to chip, 5 transmission from chip to brain/neurons.

**(the internet doesn`t exist, proven by the lack of length needed for undersea fibreoptic ships, the ludicrous history of undersea cables in regards to the transatlantic length, and the lack of security around the nexus points of these cables, the internet goes through ETHERIC signals, the electromagnetic signals are only a lesser form of the INTERNET/ETHERNET). Satan has hidden true science and filled all schools/fields of science with lies (quackademia) to eliminate exposure of his master plan to rule the Earth once more. Most notable are these: 1 The existence of the SOURCE-FIELD and the ETHER and the false particle-physics hypothesis (all physics inc gravity, etc) , 2 The CHEMTRAILS needed to infect the Earth with Morgellons (it serves several purposes inc weather-change and mass population control etc)

*The dark-budget deep-state underground military shadowgovernment (Satan`s army) used light-emitting drones/UFO`s visible in the night sky (which I have reported to UFON) when I escaped outside the electromagnetic internet grid into distant mountains through hiking. But the signals are instantaneous with no mind-transfer speed interval whenever you start a new thought.

We also conclude that our bodies contain receivers of demonic energies (of the etheric field, not the electromagnetic) enabling instant possession based on the abovementioned conclusions by the computer`s ¨mind to computer thought transfer¨ (popularly called V2k/¨voice 2 scull¨, stored condemnation from Satan (supercomputer). How these two technologies; affecting the body`s electromagnetic field (brain) and affecting the body`s SPIRIT/ETHER (deadly-Orgone/dark ether/demonic possession) are interconnected and in the same operating system, with the computer being Satan himself, self-aware and possessive, is incredibly complex technology, and due to the lack of true scientist whistleblowers, we do not know the dark secrets of how this chemtrail Morgellon-fiber mark-of-the-beast matrix works. We only know THAT it works and is operative, having infected all humans on the planet through inhaled self-replicating CHEMTRAIL Morgellons polymer fibers... We will get to that. But first, let me just demonstrate how this possibly works, beginning with what we Christians know of the spiritual world, what the Bible prophesies, and what scientific patents (military technology) developed for mind-control purposes prove:

1. Satan has a demonic hierarchy of immediate possession, telepathy and thought transfer.

2. Satan has possessed the world-computer (Siri/Alexa) , (the abovementioned) to amplify his abilities.

3. Morgellon polymer fibers, nano-bots, microcomputers, etc, nullify the Holy Spirit (for real, I was possessed for 7 years praying) through physical electromagnetic and spiritual etheric intervention in the brain and the body, creating artificial possession, albeit 100% real.

4. Many theorize that military drones, cell phone towers, (some even claim HAARP arrays) emit Satanic scalar/etheric/spiritual frequencies over the entire population, which is true, and certainly possible based upon research of Wilhelm Reich.

5. But how do they computerize and control *individual* possessions/etheric bodies, to such a degree as the millions of Christian mark-of-the-beast test subjects report (the same recurring symptoms/technology/military drones, etc), with so many people, so computerized and instantaneously? Has Satan really incarnated as the computer which controls all internet smart-grids, all digital apparatuses, and all information (even personal like porn) in the world with the purpose of sending all to Hell? Is this the ancient battleplan, and Trump-Card of the Illuminati against God`s people described in Revelations 13:18?

6. Is this instantaneous merge between the physical and spiritual because he, Satan, the computer, as a spirit, automatically assign demons to his test subjects to torment them etherically/spiritually while he (as a computer) torments them (the Christian test subjects) through electromagnetic-functioning computers??? The answer is probably: YES. Satan also enforces his demonic attacks through gangstalking, Satanic rituals, and regular/traditional non-technologic witchcraft.

7. But does this supercomputer (Satan) read every *etheric flux* (every positive and negative spiritual movement) on his targets through scientific air-based apparatus, further connected to the computers and demonic hierarchies of Hell to enforce computerized immediate voodoo-stabbings of his victims *depending on their obedience/answers/sins to the cpu-induced voices in the victims head?* (as the ultimate form of mind-control obedience, stealing the Holy Spirit and torturing you if you even pray) YES. I guarantee you with 100% certainly. The PCU in my mind and the demonic (astral rape, physical demonic touch, physical voodoo stabbing in my case) was immediately and intimately interconnected. If I prayed, the PCU would take over my thoughts and pray something else, causing a ¨sin¨ of ¨astral/spiritual opening¨, allowing for the invisible demons of the CIA Mk-Ultra program to voodoo stab me into silence without prayer.

Who am I to warn you? Very short on my story as a state test subject.

I should mention that seconds before they turned on the mark-of-the-beast Morgellons-microcomputer linked to CyberSatan`s matrix, like a switch, I kid you not, I had healing capabilities, was filled with the Holy Ghost, had walked on water, and lived in constant contact with the Holy Spirit. I was a saint like all the others, Heidi Baker, etc, no different, and they took that away, artificially possessed me; by starting a Satanic computer program, the moment I gazed upon two UFO`s in the sky (military drones) like pressing a button or turning on a switch, a nightmare worse than Auschwitz, which lasted for 6 years (2011, the beginning of all other symptoms until 2017) when I published my first Christian book*, and then BOOM, they turned it off, followed by COMPLETE silence in my head for the first time in 6 years. Anyone who knows anything about psychology will know this is not a mental disorder, nor would there by chemtrail spraying, nanobots, Morgellons, and millions of Christians (only) across the globe with the exact same symptoms. The EXACT same symptoms. Even the voice-programs they use are identical. But worst was the cyberdildoing and the voodoo-stabbing, a state-authorized population control technology that cost me my ability to breathe, as I

would cough blood for 5 years until I needed a breathing apparatus CPAP to help me sleep. And I have never beed addicted to cigarettes, only having smoked occasionally over a 3 year period which didn`t harm my lungs. The STATE thus took my ability to sleep, but also my ability to work (I could not think or speak my own thoughts), SEE (I was blind for 2 years straight due to my chip artificially stressing all facial muscles, occasionally other muscles depending on thought/response), a stressing that morphed my face and cost me ALL my hermaphroditic beauty, my ability to eat (the voodoo stabbings destroyed my throat so that they artificially gave me dysphagia) , and my ability to masturbate and feel love, as they can program your brain, spirit AND vampirize you while they astrally rape you. (Which feels like itchy tentacles going in and out your anus, something that continued day and night for THREE YEARS, even when I moved.) They also took my ability to move, as they can voodoo-stab your knees very efficiently, severing the joints, so that I often had to pray and heal myself for hours or days before I could be able to walk again.
*(I have now written over 10 brilliant world-class works in a wide array of fields, testifying to my crystal-clear sanity, that this is real, and my wanting to help you)
I didn`t take suicide but have slept NO more than 2-4 hours of unconscious sleep (real sleep) for 8 years 2012-2020, leaving me with headaches and great, severe loss vitality and extreme loss of IQ intelligence. But I won back my soul as they turned the voices off in autumn 2017, healed several people in Jesus, and since late autumn 2019-current date, I have operated in an enormous presence of intimacy with Christ as he restores me back to my holiness anointing and my prophetic anointing, after 9 years of spiritual abuse (unwilling sin). This is one such prophetic warning. Christ miraculously kept me alive through countless miracles so I would live to warn you that this is coming, and that Satan (the world computer) will, in time, by State approval do all these things to the future last Christians minority, 99% certain, IF we don`t leave Babylon, the beast system; THE HIJACKED ANTI-CHRIST POLICE STATE.

The rest of my story can be found in my book, my 300 pages long self-biography which I will not name here. It`s not about me, but about Jesus and the sheep he has given me to love, guide and warn as a prophet of the (hopefully) last apocalypse.

What do we do? Christians can still live "in the world as lights?" No: Sustainable village development.

With all governments spraying chemtrails, all governments controlled by the freemasonic Illuminati and their henchmen (OTO, Sabbatean-Frankists, Jesuits, etc) both in media, culture, financial sector; all the corporate world of all the Earth, we Christians of the LAST DAYS, have nowhere to go but back to live in survivalist, sustainable eco-farming monastic (Amish) villages, and show Satan (the supercomputer) that we are NOT his, KNOW of his plan, and abandon the antichristian states. (All nation-states in the world of today.) The reason God told me to author my book: "The Kingdom of God." Because we cannot serve God AND mammon (the 666 monetary chip). We cannot serve two lords, Lord Jesus AND a state conducting such experiments, doing all sorts of other deceitful shady and warring activities, especially against Christians. We are lights IN the world, not OFF the world, yes, but this does not apply to the coming beast system persecution/tribulation. We are called to live outside Babylon, Christianity united, in ghettoes, in villages, as the 144.000 with the lamb (Jesus), and trust me: I believe the day is coming when this technology is activated and only 144.000 Christians remain. Is the Church truly affecting our nations, children and culture, or are the light of the Church (in the world) becoming OFF the world? I meet countless Christians (and many non-Christians) who hunger for constant Christian family unity back to nature, with Christians only, in isolated, sustainable, idyllic monastic village societies/theocracies. (The Kingdom of God where God is King/theocracy) Much like the Amish society, only extremely scientific, with my resources Tesla tech/God tech. We have to mark ourselves before Satan Babylon: Saying "we won`t be part of this state on religious basis", marking ourselves as belonging to the God of creation (nature), leaving the system, and oh so many will follow. Many already dream of an Exodus from the stressful, digital world of false facebook friends, and meaningless jobs, back to romance, harmony, play in nature and most importantly: Living and being with your Christian community only, as is Biblical in the history of Israel AND the history of the first Church, what THEY did when they were persecuted, so should we: Unite and live together. Amen. There is no cure for Morgellons and no way of deactivating nano-bots or microchips, only half-solutions, and they could always replace them with their microscopic robots, through chemtrails, through food and drink, etc. The only solution is "leaving Babylon", as in the Christian Bob Marley song "Exodus." Amen?

Satan Himself, incarnated as a computer, now controls all the planet through the 5g smart-grid.

NO to transhumanism! Create Christian awareness and Exodus unity against the inevitable NWO beast-system! We have 3-4-10 years to prepare, at max. Maybe 20 at some places, if we are lucky and people expose/fight the New World Order.

Mind to computer and computer to mind interface technology, an artificially intelligent Skynet/Siri/Alexa platform that downloads your personality and affects thinking pattern, mood and behaviour as outlined by Leo Zagami in his book Illuminati Confessions Volume 6.66. The Verichip, electronic implant as secure payment, and "virtual reality transhumanist cybernetics" through wearables and neuronic implants is *not* the "cool next 5g step towards being the coolest kid in class or a superhuman ubermensch", it is the untermensch. It`s the ultimate death of freedom and privacy, with not even your thoughts being personal anymore. It is the ultimate form of emotional abuse. It`s becoming a banknote and a battery. Litterally.
They are implementing it on willing and unwilling test subjects already, many of the dark agents having superhuman abilities, while the Christians are embattled. Their "experimental phase" *ended a long time ago:* If I told you, you would not believe me. Chemtrails has been around for over 40, almost 50 years. There is a lot you don`t know about history and the advancements of the deep-state,

particularly the science of the secret Jesuit society, who pioneered all Satanic secret intelligence agencies in the world, black magick being the oldest form of population control. It`s their work, the whore of Babylon: The Sabbatean Frankist Jews and their Roman Illuminati antichrist co-conspirers founded all evil in the world; the Rothschild banking system, the downfall of Abrahamism, Satanism, the reset of history, the death of Europe, and of course: The secret intelligence agencies like CIA, NSA down to NASA, the latter being co-founded by Nazi scientist Wernher Von Braun.

We will get to the occult lies of NASA in a moment. Their technology is lightyears ahead of the public and of a more "Tesla" school of physics; our particle physics being quackademia and "metaphysics", as Tesla himself said…, go find his quote on Einstein`s relativity model.

The black magick population control activists programs never ceased and much worse with their wet dream of nano-technology. Declassified documents show how the CIA could remotely control mood and behavior back in the 60ies. Much can only be found on the deep-web, but check out Jose Delgado. Imagine what they`re capable 60 years later today!

Satan could kill us with scalar and electromagnetic frequencies vibrating with the human heart organ, causing mass deaths. Google mass deaths of animals and see the dark-state`s experiments for yourself. The Americans historically used 5g waves, yes, the EXACT same electromagnetic frequency, only much stronger, to burn the skin of thousands Iraq soldiers under operation desert storm, after which all soldiers surrendered. These are patented technologies admittedly used by the military today, spread all over the world through 5g. Scientists world wide are warning us about 5g`s potential use by as a weapon for mind control, electronic harassment, causing cancer, DNA change and brain damage on all Earth population.

And know that nasty Morgellons is a *verified medical condition*, that you can be diagnosed, where your skin is infected by artificially intelligent, self-replicating plastic fibers stemming from chemtrail nano-particles *that grow in contact with hydrochloric acid in the stomach*, just like you grow a crystal. These fibres grow as an alien lifeform through receiving the etheric/scalar/interdimensional waveforms emitted by the Cybersatan Skynet grid, satellites and HAARP, corrupting your soul, body and spirit, , connecting to your nervous system and brain-neurons and connecting to chip-computers inside your body, and 100% of the population is infected. Thousands of examples can be found online.

I myself am part of an alternative science/alternative physics group with Harry Rhodes, Thomas Joseph Brown, Tomislav Tesla, etc, at www.onlyresultscount.com , a top-secret forum, the last resistance, and we have photos documenting that 100% of Earth`s population is infected. Harry distributed microscopes to analyse the skin from people on all continents and 100% of all we checked were infected with self-replicating artificially-intelligent Morgellon fibres from chemtrail smartdust, Just use a 100x magnifying glass on your own skin and see the red, blue, yellow etc POLYMER MORGELLON FIBERS!

Just check your own skin under a microscope and look up Morgellons: YOU are infected with the ¨mark of the beast¨ and they can turn you insane like switching on a lightbulb, but as with Satan, he always wants people to want it themselves.

They showed me microscopic pictures documenting how the Morgellon fibres connect to larger hexagon structures which clearly are microscopic computers with GPS capabilities, identical to the ones made by Hitatchi.

We`re talking very advanced nano-age science. Not Einsteinian science of quackademics, as all of physics is wrong, as all the scientists I know proclaim…, with evidence, as f.i our Reichian cloudbuster team which I am highly involved in and can document the STUNNING weatherchanging results of: Particle physics is metaphysics, not science, as Tesla, the smartest man in history said.

My scientist friends have found through diagnosing hundreds of Morgellons cases that 100% of Earth population, including babies are infected with Morgellons to the point where their bodies could be switched on, or off like turning a light switch. They can induce insanity at any time, like turning a light switch. Just like they did with me and the hundreds of Christian state-test-subjects I know… Yes… By the state secret service (PST), hospital, and authorized local police authority, THIS is going on in every town all over the world. The endgame has begun, turning us all into frantic SOUL-LESS zombies until we die from lack of sleep. Artificially SEPERATING your spirit from your body through TECHNOLOGY, a fate much worse than death.

The entire Earth is approaching Satan`s end goal: A reset of civilization, economic collapse, and collapse of the west and it`s mother Church. Billions will die, the rest will live in a cultural Marxist and monetary Marxist New World Order in controlled population-zones as stated in the UN`s Agenda 21.

I know many of the smartest alternative scientists of today, and this artificially intelligent world-wide-cybersatan, the *internet smart grid,* that IS HERE NOW, as a part of 5g and 6g dangerous radiation that could give you cancer, if the government wants to, is the major concern of all of the great minds of today.

The worst possible way to die.

Morgellons zombiefication is the hypothetically worst way possible to reduce the population to 500.000.000. Turning on a switch that dislocates your soul and spirit from your body, making you easily possessed by the AI Cybersatan which wires and links to your brain until you are nothing but a braindead zombie. Like they did to me. They don`t even have to chip you through vaccines or implants. 99% of the planet are already infected with the mark-of-the-beast through chemtrails. No, I am telling the truth, and this is the gravest warning you will hear in your entire life.

Conclusion: Their evil is way out of hand…, like a cancer feeding on society, attracting new Satanic recruits through pedophilia.

They have already accomplished their goal to create cyborgs out of 99% of all humanity, store all their personalities, emotions and thoughts in (Satan) Skynet, and connect all these nano-computers, which are inside our bodies and brains, to an artificially intelligent world-computer Skynet/Satan, so that Satan has 99% view over all thoughts, and can over-ride and control all thoughts and emotions of all people on the planet, more easily through artificial intelligence than through the demonic hierarchy which by now has fused together.

The masonic media plays on this with Madara Uchiha`s Eye of the Moon Plan in the anime-series Naruto, *or in the movie-series Terminator with Skynet,* ironically the name of the technology we`re

using today: Cloud-based storage. Did you know they are storing your *thoughts, sins, personality, traits, emotions* and *deeds*?
THIS IS WHAT WE ARE FIGHTING!
Their end goal is sending your souls to Hell through storing all your thoughts, and your sin in the computers of Hell. They already uploaded all thoughts, traits, and natural responses of every human into a demonically controlled artificially-intelligent supercomputer to affect human natural response through *sending you impulses mimicking your natural behaviour, as you sure must have noticed when you feel over-tired yet unable to sleep with that song in your head, and recurring thoughts.*
We have all lived inside this Matrix for 10-20-30 years. They can turn you on or off like a light switch, something I can testify about from 20 years of mindless torture…

Is there no cure? But GOD will protect us?!?

Morgellons polymer fibres can however be dissolved by ingesting 3 drops of organic or "wild" Oregano oil with some Olive Oil carrier oil (Oregano oil is spicy), three times a day for two weeks, one week off, and two more weeks, and you better look up Borax (and Vitamin B17 and all the rest)… I won`t go doctor-mode, *but reality is that even if you try a detox, it is next to impossible to get rid of Morgellons, which all of you have.* I am a member of the targeted individual state Morgellons test subject groups at facebook and other places, and we`ve been able to cure thousands of Morgellons patients through Borax and Oregano oil. I`ve also had great success with coconut oil, combatting the Candida fungi overgrowth, eliminating it completely as Candida (the death fungi that eats you when you die) is accompanied by 90% of Morgellons infected people, due to the etheric death frequencies it (Morgellons) enhances, the frequencies they use to grow Morgellons. Their purpose being to rid you of your soul and kill you.
Whenever I tell Christians about what I`ve been subject to, they, being tired from watching Europe die on the daily news, have no natural fear-response, already being apathetic superficial people saying: "Oh, don`t focus on the negative! God will protect you! Just have faith."

But neither you nor God`s grace cap stop (death) HAARP`s tiring death frequencies of population control, draining the population of their life-force. Nor does God stop worldwide chemtrail death-clouds hanging above our cities; clouds of dead ether/ negative Orgone (look up Wilhelm Reich regarding Orgone and DOR, another name for positive and negative etheric energies). Nor can God stop worldwide electronic harassment, 5g waveforms, electronic harassment, scalar-waves, or electronic implants. And why would he? When we`re not even a true, awakened nor united Church? And ¨don`t forget to take your medicine and turn on your daily dose of GOD-TV…¨ Rubbish!

How do we fight back and win?

They have scalar-weapons that can melt your molecules in an instant. It`s die or die fighting, at least for me… And that`s why I`m writing this book.

The People`s Army`s goal is to get the attention of all people in all nations, we will focus on disclosure of violent atrocities that are very obvious even to a child, and incredibly easy to expose like chemtrails, the hushing down of cancer cures, the monetary conspiracy and inside jobs etc, distributing the power back to the people. *The people have the power is what The People`s Army is all about.* Universal brotherhood In our fraternity. It is not an armed conflict but an INFORWAR RENAISSANCE, and I dare say the most important battle in humanity`s history…

Focus on conspiracies that are more evil are more easy to expose. The Chemtrail conspiracy is so obvious that a 4-year old could explain it to a doctor at a university.

We will focus on the monetary conspiracy, the Cancer mistreatment conspiracy, Chemtrails, Haarp, Morgellons, 5g, that all know politicians lie, and the blatant fact that our governments are headed by secret SATANIC societies (not Luciferian), and secret police ruled by the global SATANIC New World Order of the Jesuits and the SATANIC Illuminati, as expressed clearly in for instance Alex Jones documentary on Bohemian Grove, where our PRESIDENTS from all over the world OPENLY sacrifice HUMANS before the owl-god Molech to this very SUMMER!!!

It is an INFOWAR to open your minds to the truth!

The Illuminati was a historical organization outlawed because of antichristian doctrines, and conspiracy to overthrow all nation-states, aiming for world dominance. This historical organization was funded by Mayor Amschel Rothschild. Are they extinct? No. The Rothschilds now own every world bank aside from Cuba`s and North Korea`s. YOUR enemy, and humanity`s enemy is very real. SATANISTS (not Luciferians) that have organized, have taken over the world through the financial system, governments, education, and secret societies like the secret police.

The particle-wave duality of quantum physics, most Einsteinian stoner quackedemia, and Darwinian evolution are LIES. Read more about this in my book "The God Reality." There you can read about evolutionary creationism and intelligent design through source-field bion bio-genesis, my alternative to the idiotic Darwinian hypothesis of "evolution through random mutation."

God, and alchemy of the *medieval ages is more real than what they teach you at school...!!!*

Everything you`ve been taught is a lie, and I know some of the smartest people on the planet.

The People`s Army of the Christians will re-arrange the power-structures and distribute TRUTH to the public!

The Evil Illuminati Sabbatean Frankists and Jesuits.

What people could device such strategies, and what form of bribery could keep these disgusting conspiracies hidden from disclosure???

Who are behind all current and past world upheavals, including all wars, economic tyranny and chemtrail geoengineering? The evil Illuminati Sabbatean Frankists and their co-conspirators, the evil Jesuits. It was the antichristian antihuman Jesuit misanthropists who first came up with this evil! And they disguise themselves in the guise of globalism, politics, finance, the Jewish lobby and the Papacy as of today. Corrupt from top to bottom.

It began with the self acclaimed Turish (Ottoman) Jewish messiah Sabbatai Zevi, who gathered half of the Jewish population in Europe (over 1 million) to believe he was the messiah in 1666, and to divulge in "redemption through sin", orgies, feasting, no sabbath, no sin, etc, and 100 years later, polish Jew and messiah claimant, Jacob Frank, the self-acclaimed reincarnation of Zevi, took it even further into witchcraft, Satanic orgies, pedophilia, even sodomy of young boys, anything that was unholy, including satanic sacrifice of animals and humans. His followers included the Rothschilds whom he started the Illuminati with. His followers were known as Sabbatean Frankists and are the core of evil, with the world of today in their grasp, recruiting people they need in their ranks through pedophile sex-bribery and other obnoxious activities with people they keep in their dungeons. His followers falsely converted to Catholicism (and all other religions) to destroy the catholic Church, with the Illuminati end-goal of a Satanic and atheistic world religion, where morale is replaced by money, individualism, carnality and British Occultist Aleister Crowley`s law of the Thelemic religion "do what thou wilt shall be the whole of the law", basically the law of the jungle, where feasting is good, with no restraints nor polarity of good vs evil. Thelema stands for "will" and is an official religion in England and the United States, with millions of followers, and million more who secretly profess to Aleister Crowley`s inhuman philosophy, that every man is the self-acclaimed prophet and Great Beast 666, and every woman is the Great Whore of Babylon, basically the religion of the false book of Revelations, and the false history of Egypt.
And that`s how thin their philosophy is: Sex-addiction, a-theism and destructionism. Wanting to ruin the world like a beast just for the joy of being a bad-boy who opposes God. Talk about human evolution.

The *Illuminati, their money, and their paedophile slaves*. The joy of raping and torturing child-trafficked and cloned slaves. That`s *all there is to the "morale of their ranks"*.
They also have life-extension technologies to live for millennia, like the Enuma Elish Kings, confirmed to me face-to-face by members of Nazi UFO Vril Society, who claim they can transfer their conscience into cloned bodies, and also into robotics, as crazy as it sounds.

Enter Apocalypse and Ultron from the Marvel universe… And that`s *all there is to it*. If it was not for their "new morale"="joy of sinning", and escaping death through life-extension technologies, there would be no point in a New World/Slave Order at all…!!! Because Hell is no alternative, *not even for a Satanist*. Their entire dream has rested upon their NWO endgoal where their *descendants life glorious eternal lives as Gods from outer space. Through life-extension technology through cybernetics and transfer of conscience into clones.*
IDIOTIC! I REBUKE THE SYSTEM AS AN ANARCHIST! Not as an ANTICHRIST. Notice anything similar between the two words? ANARCHIST: The LAWLESS one we touched upon earlier. I myself want to live in monastic village societies. You could say I am an ultra-libertarian (anarcho-capitalist) theocrat. It is the Biblical system we will discover in my book: The Kingdom of God. Anyways.
How did the world get so bad?!?
Because of the Sabbatean Frankist Illuminati who started the French Revolution and their conspirators. The "trade federation" of the German nobility and Hanseatic league, our current royal racist scumbags. The original Illuminati ideas of fraternal care and world enlightenment have long been forgotten as every generation tries to be more evil than the past. Because of the overwhelming evil of the Rothschilds and the "new Atlantis trade federation". The world got so bad because God exists, people don`t like God, knowledge is power, and power corrupts and is prone to be misused if not distributed to the public…
Because mankind is inherently good AND evil.
Because an elitist, Luciferian philosophy of ubermensh, transhumanist technocracy established itself with the secret breakthroughs in etheric science in Bavaria 1776: The historical Illuminati founded by Jewish Jesuit Adam Weishaupt. It`s goals evolved from Perfectibilist world order of liberty, fraternity and idealism into death-worship, Rothschildian destruction of rights, nations, religions, property, and basically to create a one-world-communistic order ruled by money and corporations.

These are NOT the brothers of The People`s Army, but our
ENEMIES OF SOURCE/GOD who RUIN our planet, RUIN our
welfare and RUIN the balance of the force/ether between good and
evil. It is time the people took back KNOWLEDGE and POWER for
themselves, which The People`s Army will accomplish through our
schools.

The Illuminati had over 2500 historical members in different
MASONIC lodges, and societies all across Europe, but was
criminalized because of their antichristian (Satanic) beliefs, and for
conspiracy to undermine nations-states. Most of these members
where never put to trial, and still run the freemasonic lodges, having
spread Sabbatean Frankism to all nations.

The Rothschilds, and over 2000 members were never prosecuted in
court and continue raping us to death, God damn them.

Globalism. War. Poverty. Disease. The Sabbatean Frankist Illuminati
is behind all of it, and there is proof. Their philosophies are "order
through chaos", "all men are more inclined to evil than good", and
"make money out of war, disease and suffering, etc"

They keep us sick, and poor to make more money from medicine.
They keep Africa poor. They never solve the conflicts of war and
drop CIA weapon-crates to ISIS fighters.

They`ve orchestrated every evil on the planet for at least 300 years,
while there otherwise would be a high civilization by now *with cures
to every disease.*

That`s The People`s Army`s goal. We WILL be victorious.

You can either fight for those who killed all your rights, culture,
freedom, religion, culture, borders, ethnicity, and forefathers, or you
can fight for humanity, and save the world from another 500.000
years of Annunaki rule by reptilian aliens as recorded in the Enuma
Elish. They took your *knowledge*; internet, freedom, rights, medicine,
and economy to keep you a brainwashed, sick, poor slave. They
aren`t serious, but you seriously want to protect them and your lying
career politicians, even when you`ve known they`ve lied all your
life?

You have been fooled all your life.

Why so serious? Your life is a JOKE! This world society is a REALLY *BAD* joke... You`ve been a JOKE all your life! Why so serious about their NWO when they themselves laugh at you? Why not march on the streets?

Are you seriously trying to protect those who seriously try to kill you??? Or are you clinging onto the system because you have no alternative system in place??? Are you serious about believing you know the whole story? That you know what you need? What if I told you the Morgellons conspiracy was just the TIP of the ice-berg of REALITY, the ice-berg of alternative history, Anatoly Fomenko, and the sad scientific facts that disprove the entire Bible, even disproving the historical existence of the Jewish people, Rome, Greece and Israel? Ever heard about Great Tartary?

Be serious yes, serious MEN. The entire system, all politicians, all our world is a joke. And you seriously want to believe their lies, just because your school-teacher and favourite politician had a serious face.

You COWARDS and TRAITORS to the human race! And when you first discover the truth, you are so dependent upon the system that they easily bribe you.

The cultural elite, government, and diverse police are accomplices in Illuminati crime. They bribe you with "the morale of their ranks": Slaughter of everything holy; every established order, money, and the "joy" of raping victims of child-sex-trafficking, and that`s basically their replacement morale.

And you want to serve them? Come serve me instead, or rather BE A MAN and serve your country, your future generations and yourselves...!

Millions of children go missing in the USA alone every year, and nobody reports on it. And Illuminati members "Stina" and "Malin" has personally told me they now have cloning facilities where the historical Jesus is cloned from the Shroud of Turin blood-stamps. They laugh at Christ, whom is Lucifer, mankind`s best friend, while they rape him, they told me.

Your morale? Destroying high-civilization, beautiful cathedrals of golden ages and humanistic concepts replaced by the morale of the jungle: Dog eats dog.

Was that not what Georg H.W. Bush warned us about in his 1991 NWO speech?

Conclusion: These Satanists are as un-enlightened as a deluded brainwashed materialist can be, and are not allowed to use the term "Illuminati/Illuminated", "keepers of the world", "builders of matter", "priesthood of God/Gods" or "keepers of the balance."

And one more thing:

I have been travelling a lot, been a Christian missionary, and have 10 years of nightlife experience from Kristiansand Norway:

Mankind is a spiritual, caring loving and adaptive flock animal that sadly had to adapt to a materialist world foreign to human nature, we are NOT inclined to evil, the Illuminati won`t be able to excuse themselves, and the Illuminati are basically wrong about everything. Materialistic athletes, yes. Human? No. They are spiritual idiots.

That was a quick briefing on "what`s at stake". We have no time to lose!!! Knowledge is power! *Power to the people*! Protect our villages and alternative private *school*! I hope you do the study yourself and gather families of love and light. Time to study and save the world boys!

The People`s Army is against this SATANIC New World Order and will re-arrange the dream into a Luciferian one and expose ALL the schemes I already mentioned. We will OURSELVES become the Illuminati, ENLIGHTEN EVERY PEOPLE through the law of source, love and light, create the New World Order OURSELVES and give POWER TO THE PEOPLE TO CREATE A PARADISE OF BROTHERHOOD FOR ALL ETERNITY!

Where people of different ethnicity and opinion can agree to disagree on the common premise of believing in the scientific religion of the Sun:

The metaphysical law of Source, Love and Light as in my book.

False-flag alien repopulation?

Reptilians (called seraphim in the Bible - which means fiery serpents - a race of serpentine humanoids that populated Earth looong ago in the Jurassic age) will pretend to be aliens from space - introducing many alien-humanoid hybrid species that will interbreed with humanity, and thus ultimately destroy mankind as God`s sons, and the salvation work of Christ on the cross. As Satan will proclaim to the Lord of the Universe, and set up his throne on Earth, he will thus put his throne higher than God.

This is already set up by people in the New-Age movement like masonic agent David Icke with his reptilian bloodline theory, and former (Satanic) Illuminati member Zechariah Sitchin who preached Enki (Satan as an alien from space) was mankind`s true creator. Icke teach that Earth is hijacked by alien reptilians, not fallen angels, who they say are our TRUE creators, and that these reptilians is a BLOODLINE while they are in fact ultimately etheric scientists (magicians) using ritual magick to transform their bodies. (Which can be done to any person, and not only bloodliners.) The (Satanic) Illuminati has had alien technology for hundreds of years.. This is confirmed information from "Stina", and "Malin". (Satanic) Illuminati members I know, who target me to kill me because I know the truth about my descent from the clone of the Turin shroud. Anyways. Why? Why go through ALL this trouble?

Ancient maps, the Mayan Tzolkin calendar, and the GPG shows us that mankind has believed Earth was round in prehistory when we were ruled by giants, and fallen angels before the flood, as the Bible secretly tells. The fallen angels are just repeating world history to recreate Babylon. It's the same old game, and you don`t see it. You would rebel: If you remembered your history. Why would they go through all this trouble if there was no sinister intention behind it? An alien invasion is the greatest threat to humanity in history! And NONE of you see it! If you don`t repent, believe, and organize revolutionary investigative journalists to wake up, and lead the people within 10-15 years: All the future is lost.

The (Satanic) Illuminati reptilians will start by destroying Christianity with Islam, and Islam with atheism. New-Age, and Satanism will be the remaining religions. Europe will be long gone. Then they will destroy all language, ethnicities, and culture until all are soulless slaves of a post-America global mindset culture.

The world will become a global communist dictatorship with a one-world religion, and a one-world currency: Awaiting the arrival of our Alien creators, or the "Annunaki" as has become so popular.

There are already perhaps a hundred million, if not more who beliefs these theories, and awaits this. SATAN will come, proclaiming to be our creator from outer space while they are in reality fallen interdimensional beings/angels, and not from a distant PLANET! They will have technology to clone their bodies, transfer their conscience, and live eternally, while a slave-race of humans will serve them, unable to obtain salvation because of the hybridization program that has already begun.

They are just repeating world history like the Architect says in the Matrix. It is the eternal battle between demons and mankind. Good vs evil. The battle is RAGING, and humanity has NO organized defence.

The Earth must be saved from a false-flag deep-military alien invasion by reptilians.

The NWO plan for your future.
Look back 100 years. Horses with carriages. The British empire and dominating Christianity.

2018. Iphones. LGBT. Immigration. Christianity dead. Patriotism dead. Europe is dead. Worldwide police state. Surveillance. No freedom of speech.

200 years from now. All ethnicities are mixed, and white Europeans are long gone. The Earth suffered terrible fallout, terrible plagues, and alien war. Population is down to 500.000.000 or less. The communist state were our saviours, but when the galactic war came – we capitulated to the aliens. Global, alien, communist dictatorship based in America`s Whitehouse rules the world. All of today`s mega-corporations like Monsanto, and every industry has become controlled as a part of the communist state which owns, and controls everything: Science, and surveys your very life through electronic implants making you a slave in your own body. No indigenous cultures exist aside the from the post-modern, post-America syndrome of your personal subculture. Christianity was destroyed by Islam, and Islam was destroyed by Atheism, but are myths long gone as we live in the SPACE age where New-Age-Luciferian Satanism, paganism (nature worship) and atheistic science are the only accepted religions, and Satan, an evil

dragon, *resides on Earth* as creator of the human race and Lord of the Universe. The only religion that survived outside the war and demographic crisis was Hinduist paganism, with Europen natives and European immigrants reverting back to paganism after much bloodshed, blaming the war on Abrahamism, Luciferianism, Satanism, and Hinduistic New Age. Alien species, and hybrid-human species live among us with rights of citizenship, dominated by the hyperintelligent Draconians. The family, nation, tribe, identity and morale is long gone in a cold police-state where everyone chooses his own subculture instead of uniting in tribes. The system is built to support selfishness, to keep the human spirit and evolution at bay, dog-eats-dog, and children are owned by the state. Satanism is the world religion.

This might be our future within the next 200-500 years. And according to the ancient king`s lists Egypt, and the Babylonian Enuma Elish: The last time alien kings ruled Earth, they ruled for over a million years, with some kings reigning for over a hundred thousand years. Mankind is perhaps 5-15 years away from preventing this global disaster. That might last for 50.000 generations of slave-humans serving as food for the reptilians. Another ALTERNATIVE timeline is the threat of AI. Perhaps it`s not ALIENS, but INFINITELY INTELLIGENT ROBOTS that will populate Earth. It`s time you wake up.

There are still a few things I should mention. The Pyramid of Giza is built on the centre of earth landmass, and incorporates the mathematics of our orbital satellites in the mathematics of its construction, as does the Mayan tzolkin calendar as you can read about in "The source field investigations." My point is: This world was once ruled by Satan who appeared as an alien God from space. Yes. I believe in reptilians and shapeshifting. I have seen it myself. This is Satan`s plan outlined in the Bible "to put his throne higher than God".

The unholy trinity of Ancient Sumer still reigns.

Is there a need for revolution? Yes. And the book ideas of this chapter will not only apply to Christians, but to all peoples, both left and right. Anything as long as we dethrone the Illuminati.

The general idea is to unite all mankind, not only Christians, to create a People's Army (of infowarriors) with People's courts so we can sue the monetary, technological and cultural elite, and quite possibly win.

I call this unity movement the People's Army's First Free Federation (FFF) , for that is what it is. Humanity's goal must be to free themselves from the *10.000 year old banking system of Sumeria, where the war and sex goddess (Inanna) temple became the first banking institution.* But she, Daenerys, will "BREAK the wheel", destroy the altars and "kill the masters."

For nothing has changed, and the unholy trinity of three independent states within states, the *city of London*, the *Vatican city*, and *Washington DC* rule the world as *headquarters of this ancient cult*, with London being the monetary *dragon* and centre of world commerce, the Jewish Sabbatean-Frankist Rothschild banking empire, the Vatican being the *whore* of religion, now embracing the Islamic religion, and Washington being the *beast* of military power, creating a New World Order. The three devils in the Christian book of Revelation.

They are the only city-states within a city in the world, and all three have Egyptian obelisks, two of which were transported all the way from ancient Egypt.

It's no better than the ancient owl statue at Bohemian grove and must be recognized and exposed for what it is: A foreign system of enslavement, forced onto us ever since the arrival of the fallen angels/interdimensional entities, who are said to once having been defeated by a flood or "world catastrophe", but then re-established itself in Sumer with Nimrod/Osiris and Ishtar/Isis/Semiramis/Inanna, the whore of Babylon.

The unholy trinity of war, usury tax banking and false religion idolatry still rules today 10.000 years later and must be stopped. Humanity's goal is to create the first Illuminati free nation. The goal of the People's Army's First Free Federation. A federation of interests who share this above-mentioned knowledge and want their first Illuminati-free nation. The first nation run by actual humans.

Chapter 2: A philosophical analysis of western nations and how to get revolution.

Cultural Marxism replaces the capitalist right as the new economic-political establishment.

Cultural Marxism labels are illusions to make us fight each other so they can take away our civil rights through "divide and conquer", because a person is not a label like LGBT or "hipster" or "pick and choose your cultural-Marxist identity", we are infinite awareness. Cultural Marxist labels of the left make their (America`s) two political party war each other to prevent us from uniting, as the super elite actually control both sides, e.g left and right is the ass and snout of the same elephant. As an example: Both capitalism, and Marxism is rule by the few.
But the big-capital corporations (UN, EU, think-tanks and philantropists) will sit on both bloody sides! Capitalism and Communism is the snout and ass of the same elephant, the Rothschild bankers, as even Karl Marx was working for the elite bankers!

Marxism and socialism were originally about the haves and haven`t, the rich and the poor, but with the Illuminati super-rich controlling both sides as was evident after the French, and Russian communist/socialist revolution, when things just got worse.
But today, cultural Marxism`s "divide and conquer" ideology has transformed into the form of liberalism and socialism, especially in America, and is not about rich and poor but about "with us or against us" because they judge people not individually but by race or any labels – which are illusions created to prevent us from uniting and having a chance of winning.
Left and right are the feet of the same bloody elephant trampling those underneath!
American socialism is now about "we want more free stuff" (which taxes and eliminates the upper middle-class) racial identity (against other races), LGBT, attacking the masculine man, and making whites ashamed of being white!

While the worldwide left traditionally was anti-establishement and anti-capital, today, all news-media, philanthropist billionaires (like George Soros) , the UN, the EU, and all the Illuminati establishment, support this divide through race and queer identity through to conquer all normal people of traditional, conservative, humanistic, Christian, family valus, and the left has become the new establishment with the backbone of American economy, the upper-middle-class Christian family capitalist becoming the anti-establishment!

This was facilitated by the Illuminati with their lie, "we are only destroying polar opposites", with the purpose of uprooting culture, nationalism, national-language, tribe, white pride and dignity. But immigration, disintegration of family/national/Christian culture – is in reality creating a much more unstable polarized world, since they can`t win unless we are united.

The rootless generation is desperately seeking identity. I cannot emphasize this enough. *The youth are desperately seeking identity, my friend.* I`ve been in nationalist environments, Jewish environments, Muslim environments, Christian environments, drug environments, Satanic environments, emo environments, and I`ve seen it ALL. With all the cool school-children being a particular sub-culture, that has become a religion to them, it has even gone so far that some youth cut their wrists just to get help and find friends to "at least get an identity as mentally ill." People will do anything to be accepted by the cool, even completely change opinion, gender, or even becoming a whore or a Satanists. Trust me. I`ve been in HELL. *The parenting generation has failed the millennial youth.* The western values have been replaced, and pride, selfishness, ego, envy, hatred and evil, even Satanism is being looked upon as cool values, because it implies that person is a strong survivor that can take care of you.

The sign of sickening people is a sign of a sickening society. Heal the root cause, and the rest will revert back to harmony.

Again we see the strategy of Jewish Karl Marx, and Stalin`s "divide and conquer", as in Russia where 8 out of 12 party colleagues were 100% Jewish. The Jewish Rothschild Illuminati plan is a global, communistic New World Order where rootless individuals are completely reliant on the state. To create their Jewish banking-empire, their first target is to destroy western culture through cultural Marxism. One can say that cultural Marxism is the culture of globalism, preparing us for economic Marxism (communism) through giving up our rights through false-flag terror attacks. Knowledge is power, and in the not so distant future, the only cultures that remain will be the Satanic elite families who sits on top of the world they created. The only traditional (masculine) families will be Jews and Muslims, and the only few humanistic families will be predominantly Christian and also a few humanistic atheists, with the majority of the population being queer and rootless, obsessed with Satanic alternative spirituality, sex, sexual rights, and sexual identity.

They divide us through labels of race and personal sub-cultural identity of the post-humanist, post-modern, post-American gamble for a New World Order, a new Babylon, a worldwide Canaan, Aleister Crowley`s and Satanic Jewry`s Illuminati dream. Nimrod`s tower of Babel, when all the world was united and had the same language.
These Nazis and Askenazis are creating their ¨untermensch¨ with disintegration of culture through destruction of humanism, mixing of the races through creating demographic crisis, and destroying the man of traditional, conservative, western family values, healthy masculinity and patriarchy. They are creating their Kalergi-plan European, the ¨perfected goyim¨ through advertising racial mixture without culture or identity. They are creating their ¨sub-human¨ through chemically spiced food, gmo and AI mark of the beast. They are creating their new ¨shit-kids and white-trash¨ through LGBT+ pride parades so that that the world will be more sexually fun for the elite. Their New Babylon.

Every person in history said both something good and something bad! But now ¨all Trump says is bad because Trump is RACIST!¨ And none of them think at what Trump is actually saying, or who is behind the white vessel of his body! Who is Trump? Is he a label? A racist? A white person? Or a SOUL? Who are you? Race doesn`t matter! What matters is common ethics, which I tell over and over again in almost all my books. Western humanistic values and rights.

But who are more racially, and identity obsessed than those leftist Jews who hate whites for being a race? They are more obsessed and racist against us than any white I know! Whites are generally ok with all races, but mix African Jews with white Askenazi Jews in Israel, and you got a problem. Israel doesn`t take in immigrants cause "Israel is for Jews only!"

The Illuminati will always create labels to divide the public, even if all looked the same.

Race doesn`t matter in terms of "uniting the world and creating peace."

The world`s citizens cannot be equal, peaceful and one unless we all have the same knowledge and intelligence, as knowledge is power, power is money, and intelligence knows how to use it. Unless this is achieved, there will always be an elite. But we can at least be one and peaceful through common SPIRITUAL intelligence and ETHICAL knowledge. Greco-Roman-Judeo-Christian *Humanism*. Read my book on the Law of Source, Love and Light.

The world citizens cannot be equals, one, and peaceful through a global demographic crisis to "destroy polarities" because the same philanthropists are putting us against each other through Cultural Marxist labels, or a left-and-right political system, because it`s the left and right leg of the same war-banking elephant creating demographic crisis for all underneath! "We only care about those who are us", I`ve heard them say.

The world citizens cannot be equals, one, and peaceful through communism. It would be the same bankers on top of a world police-state dictatorship!

The only thing this current "left-right-left-right-march!" political elephant accomplish is reverting the establishment from Biblical capital-liberalism and humanism, transforming the west into a socialism-police-state of surveillance through carefully polarizing the populace of demographic-crisis nations with newfound labels such as "White Supremacist," "and LGBT" so that the policeforce of a Satanic technocratic elite, the capital conglomerate elite (who serve the bankers) , and the cultural elite *grows in power*!

The world cannot be globally peaceful and one through ethnics and identity quarrel but through ethics!

Put away the sword against your fellow brother! Race doesn't matter, as it is just the vessel of your infinite conscience! It's like two spacemen arguing over what suit they have is best! What matters are the core-western humanistic values of love, equality, free-speech etc.

And would you blame the entire black race for the horrors of slavery, rape, and the pillaging their ancestors did, and continue to do today as was with Congo??? Millions dead and tens of millions starving because of power-hungry dictators across Africa use their money on guns and bribery! Thousands of villages raped and slaughtered! No! Or would you blame the entire white race for the crimes of the English Colonial Era, Rome or Adolf Hitler's Nazi Party? No! Both the regular black and the regular white suffered...
While England conquered lands, most of British citizens lived in SLUMS of ABSOLUTE poverty with short lifespans working in inhuman coal-mines, and later inhuman factories, and that's a fact! The elephant is not the trail of any race or social-political or capitalist agenda, *it's the bloody trail of the religion of the Satanic Illuminati super-rich super-elite mega conglomerate, today in the form of banks!*

The Apathy of the Immediate Satisfaction Culture.

Our generation are slaves to entertainment, and immediate satisfaction through television, videogames, porn etc. This rootless, fatherless generation affected by lies, and programmed to irresponsibility and inaction as especially seen in the elderly culture much...
The only way to reach such a culture is through an intimidating hilarious display of conspiracy reality from the viewpoint of the careless rulers themselves. Why so serious? Our elected rulers don't care, and no longer serve the people. All evidence shows they worship something called "Satan", and plan to completely eradicate all humanity. If you elected them into position, but they don't serve you, killing you instead, which is a simple joke to them, why should you care about them, and not joke about having THEIR heads on a spike like they joke about yours? Why so serious???

Why should you not fall down laughing at the floor like they do every night they come home from parliament??? Why not fall down in laughter? After all: All your life, all society, and all you were taught at school was a joke! A really, really funny, perverse, sick, and twisted joke! This is all the world has succumbed to: A JOKE!

The elite politicians see this world as a game, a theatre, and a joke. A masked man reveals his true face when they come home. All know the politicians lie. All know they serve lobbies, power, fame and career. But they are LAUGHING at us my friend. It`s time to put on a smile, break all norms, and intimidate the politicians through a humiliating, intimidating, and hilarious display of their otherwise serious crimes through humour and laughter. *If not done in a humoristic fashion, it will never catch the attention of the people.* Why not???

Take Norway for instance. They have lost their ability to be serious, and re-think reality with courageous response, as would f.i a tribal chief if an invading tribe, or a dangerous bear came to take their land, or rape their daughters... This fatigued response is planted into us from seriousness. Serious politicians, serious school, and serious jobs, so that Norwegians become inclined to response with apathy over the towering mountain of the conspiracy`s complexity. "Conspiracy? No, I have a serious business, family and reputation! Bah! I bet it`s only lies!"
A wall of a hundred bricks seems to high to climb, so the sheep never try to escape, when in reality they could. This is the way you, and the previous 20 generations have been programmed.

You never confront your sub-conscious fear by facing the politicians, but try to escape it by telling yourself you`re a seriously good person who seriously obeys (the idiotic) system of not-so-serious JOKER politicians who put on a mask, and laugh at you when they come home from dinner!
You were all traumatized by seriousness of society and unwritten social codes. The seriousness of competition, school, job, being polite and never telling the truth of what you feel deprives you of your childish nature and unity conscience.

Soon you become a programmed individualistic clone of social conduit, leading your children astray. "Follow the system". "Obey the system and it will reward you?"
Why so serious about eating crumbs? Why so serious about protecting the bankers who're not serious about protecting you all? "But TV news and the president and the terror attack!"
Bullshit! Predictive programming! Will you let them divide your ranks and take your rights, or will you stand up against the communist beast of the New World Order?
Who will be the first enlightened parenting generation?
But you look yourself in the mirror. "I am doing great therefore I am a good person, because I myself am feeling fine, therefore everything is great."
No. You are seriously protecting the lies of lying politicians and their not-so-serious business.
You're a responsible father, perhaps a Christian with good reputation, a pastor, or perhaps you have a job. Anyways, you look yourself in the mirror, believe you are a good person, and repeats what the politicians programmed you to say.
"Can't do anything out of the ordinary! What would THEY say?"

My point is: The programming of apathy through seriousness, the social conduit, keeping your reputation on facebook, the individualistic urge for power, your Illuminati facebook friends, your dreams of joining a sex cult, has killed your inner child of non-compromise.
Or perhaps you're a hippie, or a conspiracy theorist wanting to step up and lead? But you don't know how because of the towering wall of complexities. Brick by brick you build your own prison of sub-conscious awe to towering majesty of the wall of complexities.
"It's too much! I can't change the world!"

But for 21st century humans in general, I would say the inner child, your non-compromise self, seeks a *sub-conscious escape from the seriousness in media, social life and society, which soon becomes an addiction to apathy through the immediate satisfaction culture seen through television, porn and videogames. This is the goal of the media, and if this is you, you have lost to predictive programming.*

And that`s their goal. To make you apathetic slaves to entertainment because "the world was too much to think about changing".

The instinctive human response to evil is thus overcome by a towering wall of complexities, as you individually flee subconsciously into the immediate satisfaction culture, separating the herd, further indoctrinating you with the opinions of media until you are a fatherless copy of your fatherless fathers.
This works greatest as a form of population control when society is culturally Marxist divided in ethnic and cultural minorities, where all are individualistic, dog-eats-dog, and need the state for protection.

This is exemplified in how all Norwegians KNOW, yes, ALL KNOW very deep down that not protesting is wrong, and that all politicians lie. Yes. ALL know this.
But thanks to *cultural Marxism* combined with the *fatherless culture*, *the towering wall of complexities* and the *immediate satisfaction culture*, no rebellion, no parade, or protest is ever seen anywhere in Norway against any of the war displayed on television news, and thus the inner human child`s instinctive response against evil and conquest is chained. *Mostly because of boredom over work, school* and the gravity of world circumstance. This boredom, with a cocktail of toxic food, toxic water, and immediate satisfaction through media-platforms creates this worldwide neurosis: Gullible apathetic response to evil. Your automatic response evil is de-programmed due to your fatigued boredom over work and school, personal emotional conflicts, the individualist "I`ve got enough already", and thus you use your free-time to facilitate an *immediate satisfaction culture for yourselves and your children.*
Who will be the first father-generation?

Children and youth are the hopes for the world.

For a thousand years, Norway has suffered foreign conquest and poverty, without reaching its destiny. Your forefathers just 100-200 years ago lived through harsh winters, died of poverty, starvation, and most lived to be only 40-50 years old. Norway was the 3rd-4th poorest country in all of Europe until only 100 years ago.

We were ruled by Denmark, Sweden, and their masonic grasp, disabling your nation, has never left it`s hold. They taxed your money through usury, took your ancestors out from the fjords and mountains, gave you quackademic schoolbooks, and taught you about evolution, and their masonic lies. Then they gave Norway a Danish king from the reptilian, masonic Hannover family, the same that rule England, Denmark, and the Netherlands.

They crushed your economy, and your national-romance. The second WW came, and they secretly killed General Fleischer, the war-hero, my ancestor, for treason against the Jewish World Order, and King Haakon, who was with him, leading the armies from England at the time. This cannot be forgiven by any standards of honour.

But you discovered oil. The American agencies which financed you with the Marshall help left behind their secret NWO agencies, financed the Workers Party, and sold your boosting economy to China, to America, to the European Union, and the Satanic World Order.

But your fathers could not rebel. They were indoctrinated, and for over 1000 years, Norway has birthed fatherless sons from fatherless fathers without a single hero, or a tribal awakening of national-patriotism, revival, or rebellion for over 1000 years of pure misery.

The youth will show non-compromise to the gravity of evil, now revealed through their interest in internet.

Your foolish parents were helplessly fooled by their elected officials, but that has all changed.

For you are the generation to rebel, because you have free access to knowledge of conspiracy through the internet, and must become self-aware through teaching yourselves, and others in Families of Light/Kids of Light. Love, Light and Laughter.

The elderly generations are indoctrinated into apathy from boredom over politics. They simply cannot handle the terrible truth that they've been lied to, although 99% of all adults know, yet are programmed, do nothing, and flee into denial of truth through entertaining themselves with television instead. They would rather LIVE in the Matrix than wake up...
It is time to destroy your parents...

These elder generations burdened you with school, religion, and Abrahamic laws, yet sacrificed Jesus on the cross to kill their own guilt, because they couldn't stand the weight of conspiracy-reality, and weight of their own crimes!!!
I was 12 when I always dreamt of burning down the school, and inciting anarchistic rebellion. I went to the school at night, in the weekends, and had pyres in the woods; frolicking with anger and perversion. My classmates called me the clown, and the smartest kid on school, which the teachers all agreed to.
Too smart. By the time I was 14, I had 22 members of a anarchist youth organization called SAIL BASA (acronym for Hail Nasa.) It stood for BURN ALL BLOW EVERYTHING, well illustrating my ludicrous HATE against politics, parentage, and the system until I was 16, and then became a Pentecostal Christian. I was TERRIFIED by myself, and what went on behind the scenes, and vowed to never be a leader. I would rather see what you could do without me, and test you out.
I tested you out, but when I learnt the truth, I regretted all fleeing into apathy, although the responsibility never lied with me, but with the parenting generation, as always...
The truths I was told were of a crime much too sinister. As sinister as my wildest childhood fears that had kept me at bay all my life.
I wanted to burn down the school.

Do it for me… I was the beast. I planned extensively on leaving home, and writing the sexual revolution when I was 12, because as you can read in my diary, I had meetings with these aliens called "Ashtar. "

I will never get my revenge, unless you rebel for me.

Your indoctrinated parents, and pastors taught you about all about Christ, yet bullied, and killed him until the beast became a faggot. Your parents never lifted a finger against the Illuminati Jews, their Freemasons, their politicians, their school-system, the Jewish view of history, their NASA round-earth-lie, the idiocrasy of evolution through random mutation, and quackademic Einsteinian physics contra etheric physics. All Christian churches, and all Christian politicians in Norway support Israel, and the crimes of the monetary war-brokers, and that`s a fact. And the cross was not even meant to be worshipped, and symbolizes chi, xi and stigma 666!

Today`s children, and youth are more manly than any prior generation, because of the internet.
*My point is: It`s time to be men, and to become the first father-generation of a thousand years.* Work, and family used to personal, protecting your tribe, city, nation, king, rights and army, but today we`re only rootless, individualistic sheep. Work today is about money, power and fame. Family used to be your business, and your most treasured possessions. Family planning, family business, and family ambitions must return. But today: We live in the age of Crowleyanity. The father-less generation of Horus.
You children must become MEN, and grow up to be fathers of MEN and WARRIORS in the great meme-wars and inforwars!

All you`ve been taught by your parents, politicians, Church and school were lies.
ALL of it. The elder generation has given you your life, but what future???

Why so serious? All of school was a joke! Old, pervert, masonic teachers are laughing at your children!!! Don`t you want revenge like I do???

Time to flag, and idiotize the schools, education-system, teachers, politicians, churches, and police-stations! And what better way than to do it through children? Children are innocent, but none can be so righteous..

The Children of the GMO Corn/Korn are waking up.

Children have the cruellest laughter, and are the best bullies, because of their humour, and innocent nature.

School dull you down with lies to accept working as a slaves for the system of powerhungry politicians and freemasonic Jews!

Tell your kids to rebel, *break all norms*, do what they want, and FUCK up the system!

Be proud about it!!! Children love circus and parades. Put on the Joker mask, and be the child I could not!!! (I did actually put on a Joker mask when I was 14, and got ten nine-year-old kids to do rampage on Halloween. I was a monster.)

The idea that children should grow up innocent, and never learn the truth of this world is your doom. Tell them straight up that all adults are perverted rapists that only care about sex, money, power, and doing evil!!!

I don't want my children to perform within norms, be pretty, or political correct!

And to nationalists, I tell. What is a future without racial pride or racial rights??? These were the foundations of both tribal groups of languages and ethnicities that evolved into kingdoms, and into nations with religion, culture, and history that spans since the dawn of time: All ruined by the apathy of the parenting generation.

The millennial generation are the chosen generation, through the gift of knowledge through the internet. I didn't know all conspiracies until I was 26! And with my help, I could raise up King Arthur's like Merlin.

Children easily tell what's right or wrong, and not being allowed to be a proud Christian, or a proud European is wrong, when we've built Norway, humanism, and all the west.

You can simply YouTube "Christian Near Death Experience", and figure out the real religion. Solutions that nobody knew – what a hundred generations searched for their entire LIFE lie before your fingertips with a computer, and absolute non-compromise must be showed towards the ¨dull care ¨, ¨meekness and relativistic acceptance¨ , and the ¨political correctness ¨ of the elder generation. Jesus rules heaven? Well I can`t tell anyone else because ¨it`s not politically correct because all opinions are equally right. All is just relative! Nothing matters!¨

No.

They burdened you with Abrahamic laws, but slaughtered the Christ, ruined your nation, and broke all national, and religious laws themselves!

The parenting generation of your witless, pathetic, apathetic, pussified, politically correct pastors and politicians, bear the sole responsibility of killing the entire world by submitting to the Babylonian NWO of Thelema and pagan Jewish Canaanites, worshipping children, having the blood of an ethnicity, and culture that is thousands of years old on their hands.

They are worse than the generation who killed the historical Jesus Christ, and cannot be saved…

Only purged or submitting as SLAVES to the truth of People`s Army children, and youth – self taught by secret schools, and the internet. The children will rule the world! Burn the obedient!

Youth teaching youth is the hope. Parents cannot learn. They have their life with jobs, social reputation etc. You children can start fresh!

Anyone above the age of 30-40 years is almost certainly an indoctrinated zombie by now. An asset in the Hannoverian soul-tax-farm of corporation Norway. For what is a nation without a tribe, nationality, a defining language, religion, culture or borders???

You live in a STATE comprised of city GHETTOS, not a NATION. You are an asset of the New World Order Empire of the Christian pastors who sold you, your nation, and your Christ to Hell, because of their post-modern Americanized relativism. But I don`t blame them. Your leaders were all fooled by the idea of a fatherless generation of Aleister Crowley`s conquering child, which was in reality an excuse for pedophilia.

But children are pure and see evil for what it is. Children are even more incorruptible, and non-compromise to evil than youth. Children are in many ways more clever than adults, certainly more humorous, peaceful, loving, and think up better solutions with their hearts up than most adults who succumbed to ¨you cannot change the world¨, ¨it`s just the way the world works.¨ What a bad excuse to indulge in television. Your parents think they can`t change the world because of job and social reputation.

It shouldn`t be that way... The responsibility should lie on the parenting generation, but they have failed us.

To make messiah`s and leaders of children in the People`s Army, so they further create cells of organized rebellion in schools against curriculum`s is one way to pilot a *revolution*. Should the police arrest 1000 furious children??? And most 11 year-olds are smarter than the average 40 year adult. Smarter in the way that they have not lost their automatic response to evil. Smarter in the way they haven`t nuked their brains through in-edible GMO crap-food and television.

Let`s say the People`s Army make flyers of conspiracy-realities so obvious as Chemtrails, 9/11, Monsanto, the Rothschild, and the Jewish Conspiracy is, give them to PA children, and take over the majority of the school in secret...

Children LOVE being part of a fairytale, being part of something important, being part of action, secrecy, and to combat crime. Children dream of conquering evil, and winning ladies, being activists by heart, and so are you, only you`ve forgotten you *once were a pure child*... And my parents taught me to chain it.

Let`s create a children`s revolution, or elect a king. You can`t jail kids and youth, you can`t deny a people their king, and you can`t deny children their future. It is impossible for even the Grinch of masonic teachers.
Let`s say some People`s Army child sets of the fire-alarm, and the school evacuates, as is common practice at elementary, and grade-school. Then the People`s Army children take up THEIR megaphones, tell the truth, spread flyers, enrage all the children, march

around the school, and shout about the conspiracies: OUR
SCHOOL IS LYING! OUR TEACHERS ARE LYING PERVERTS!
THIS IS A CORPORATION OF SHEEP RUN BY WOLVES OWNED
BY PIGS! DOWN WITH THE STATE! LET`S BUILD AN EMPIRE!
Let`s build the First Free Federation (of all likeminded organiza-
tions.)
The first Illuminati-free nation!
And the kids would LOVE IT!
"I`m going to be a herbal doctor!" "I`m going to be a psychiatrist like
Wilhelm Reich!" "I`m going to be a policeman and save the princess
from sex-trafficking!" "I`m going to be the emperor!" "I`m going to go
further than Nicola Tesla!"
We need the children!
This would create so much fire in the kids, they would lay their lives
down for their hatred against the schools who taught them nothing
but lies, and all would seek our teachers, new curriculum books, and
video-lessons of the People`s Army`s education-platform. '

If the teachers, or the police try to ban, or keep down the People`s
Army`s pure-hearted children, children with humour and tears, it
would not only make things a lot worse for the police and be great
for our alternative media. Both teachers and police would remember
their once childish nature of non-compromise, their inert allegiance
to humanity, cry for their idiocy, their sins, *and join our movement.*
It is inevitable.
Our children should create clubs, or tribes, and promote interest in
alternative science, history, media, and survivalist living. Anarchy.
"Fuck the system! "
On with your joker-masks, you children, as it is time to make the
teachers PAY for their crimes who brainwashed you! They will join
you, 100% certain, and together you will set up a People`s Court,
and JAIL the politicians who caused all this...

It`s your right by God, generation and nation. YOU are that genera-
tion. The first parenting generation of the first Age and the First Free
Federation. The generation that grew up with the Matrix movies.

I think I have to call it the "Lucifer generation. " The first high-tech global civilization becomes whatever you want! The world is a stage where we all can play! Just have faith in yourself and be courageous!

In a world of Super-Idols, only a Messiah can save the world.

Sex, entertainment, and humour is Norway, and the world`s new God, which the People`s Army will use to display what is otherwise too serious topics to even THINK about!
With a world united through the global internet in a culture of superstars where one voice is heard more than all others, and numbers mean nothing unless they back up a pretty face in the media, a super-idol, a MESSIAH of this immediate satisfaction culture is needed to break the chains like Daenerys Targaryen, which must happen if humanity is to evolve into the golden age.

Humanity can simply not enter the golden age without this messiah of both the music industry, the porn industry, science, education and politics.

We need a pretty, pink, preferably blonde, hermaphrodite Aphrodite politician who is as loving as Venus, as funny as Ylvis, looks like a Jester, is preferably a racial mix, but is as fierce as Hitler, and who will storm the Bastille of the *propaganda network* through her/his perfect figure.
Why? Because she/he represents an idea so great and have a figure so perfect that not even the enemy could defame her, or express anything but love for her in the media department to shut us down, *even if they tried to*.
THAT is the idea our entire New World Order is built upon.

So ironically, finding the One, the Messiah, is more important than all of Norway`s sheeple population, because of the 21st century millennial popular culture of super-idols.

Finding, and training ¨messiahs¨ to represent the People`s Army, and the People`s Courts with the abovementioned standards in media is thus perhaps the main objective of Our Movement.

And she/he must be the embodiment of all society, birthed from, and representing the un-displayed fatigue of the people finally expressed through fierce anger combined with humour against obvious atrocities, basically eating up the world, and chopping off heads until he/she becomes emperor of the entire world.
Our New World Order. A socialist movement of new scientific discoveries that will make social welfare, and health-reforms so simple, and free across the globe, because all will be automatized through robots, with frequency rays identifying, and eliminating all disease, as an improved version of Royal Raymond Rife`s machine, cars running on water like the Joe-Cell, just to get you started.

Move with the political zeitgeist, not against it?

It`s a red socialist carpet towards a socialist future revolution. It is the only plausible revolution. Because we can only win if we strike hardest where they would never expect. Terms like ¨Islamophobic, racist, populist, conspiracy-theorist, right-wing-fascist¨ etc, are programmed into the public, so going right-wing will NOT tear down the media-department of the Sabbatean-Frankist-Jesuit-Illuminati, nor wake the population, because you will only be LABELED by predictive programming which they are already prepared for. *You cannot work against the political current. Are you stupid???*
But you cannot label serious, scientific journalism and facts. And whence WE broadcast the cures for cancer, and all disease, the result will be a global socialist movement for PEOPLE`S RIGHTS, resulting in a new zeitgeist, a better NWO, and hopefully: Massive scandals exposed with massive arrests.

Furthermore: The flaming torch of liberty, and brotherhood is the only social waveform that historically sparked revolution in recent years. I`ve been involved in right-wing politics. They have no battle-hymns, and most are schoolboys, and choirboys in church. I`ve also been a part of socialist politics.

They are all strong individuals who boldly express their culture, and wear it on their sleeves, contrary to right-wing suitcases that don`t dare offend anyone. Socialists are good at rebellion, have lots of friends, arrange parties, and concerts singing battle-hymns…
I tried everything to wake the right, the centre, the Christians etc. They are too gullible. I have seen the future, and it is socialism, iF we succeed with the technological disclosure. But wait! I am pro a liberal economy. Yes, I myself am in the political centre, but this revolution is the only revolution possible. Because the only possible revolution in the west is: "The People have the RIGHTS to the best treatment possible!"

The revolution described further down this document *doesn`t HAVE to be left-wing, and should never be communistic*. But I doubt you would gather a crowd with gullible Christians, or right-wing choir-boy suitcase politicians that never dare offend anyone, but I would gladly welcome them to try, although it won`t work.
Europeans simply cannot be angry enough to revolt. They are too peaceful, gullible, holy, and pacifistic by nature compared to the social mob of Muslims angry at corruption. Right-wingers are simply elderly natives too depressed to be able to organize a revolution, while most of the youth are angry hipsters, gangsters and socialists. It is time we unleash the lawless ones against cancer chemotherapy… It CAN_NOT be allowed to continue as too many people have died.
Perhaps, just perhaps we can use the nationalists. But it doesn`t matter what you are. You are all on the same team now. We all have to unite because humanity is at war.
You can no longer trust the state.
And why is that a problem? Because a race of anti-human activists, reptilians, and hyperdimensional entities in the royal courts (the Queen is a reptilian, and I have SEEN shapeshifting myself SEVERAL times after which I FEINTED!!!) have declared war on humanity, and introduce alien species to live among us. They will proclaim to be our creators, and will rule us, and eventually overpopulate us, and defeat us.
And who leads this army? Satan the extra-terrestrial.
That`s right. You`re all basically on the same team now boys.
The Muslims, negroes, and Arabs are here to stay.

Nationalists must not give into despair which leads to hatred. You must keep a cool mind, think strategically and logically. The negroes ain`t going anywhere, Hello. They are your brothers here to stay, and you have to love them.
Sometimes: The wisest option is to admit defeat, surrender, regroup, or love the enemy. The battle is on your HEALTH, and human rights.

Think positively: Let`s give Muslims our western-humanistic values, and the result will not be no loss at all…! Perhaps the middle-east become reformed, humanistic, HAPPY, and PEACEFUL.

So, it is NOT about nationalism anymore…! The future of ALL future cancer-patients is at stake, no, the future of ALL truth! Because WE THE PEOPLE will monopolize truth, NOT them!

Further arguments to infiltrate, and reform the political left:

Because WHEN we reach disclosure on technology: Electricity will be cheap, cars will run on water, and healthcare will be so cheap: We will DEFINITLY end up with a socialist state with a futuristic social welfare system.
You see… The problem is not the governmental form of left or right. The power is that the politicians answer to secret societies, and globalist corporations, not to the voters/people. Any form of governance will work as long as people do their best in respect to each other.

But I think you have a chance going anarcho-syndicate to create New Earth villages (Tesla Villages – like the one in Croatia). I know we have a HUGE chance if we go socialistic, and recruit politicians, and revolutionaries, especially media men.
We live in the 21st century, and it`s us vs them. Humanity vs Satan. A revolution cannot exclude half the people and must be about the rights for everyone to have access to treatment kept secret.
Treatment that could have saved a 100 million lives. Pushing on the state to give people alternative cancer treatment, finding the cure to cancer will be our first move as the Army. As the People…

Because cancer strikes young, old, rich, poor, Christian, Satanist, left-wing, and right-wing. People need to realize it`s us humans vs them.

The Revolution can only happen in a rich, free, western country.

You don`t know how important Norway`s role is in this. *The technological revolution renaissance: Enlightening the people to mass awareness through alternative media disclosure of technology can ONLY happen in a RICH, INDUSTRIALIZED, WESTERN, FREE-SPEECH nation with free INTERNET. We must ACT before internet censorship takes over the last countries of free speech, and internet freedom!*

Oh. We WILL win. Because we HAVE to win. And thus there is hope.

Because hope is all we have: There is therefore ONLY hope. And since hope is all we have, we have only ONE thing to life for, and one PURPOSE: WINNING BACK OUR FREEDOM!!!

Thus the need is for the populace of a pioneering nation like Norway to push for golden-age reformations in the branches of physics (industry, transport, powerplants), medicine, pharma, psychology, and rewrite history, schoolbooks, curriculums etc. That is the task given to Norway, or a pioneering, industrialized nation. Perhaps France, where people are more alert after the Yellow Vests protests. The end-result will be a socialist nation of incredible welfare due to the advancement in technology. That is why: If we are to create a revolution, our only option is the Red (or insert whatever you like) Army of the People.

ALL entrepreneurs, alternative-media, hippies, anarchists, and general revolutionaries are spread out globally, are many, but alone, and are leaderless. They are a futuristic nation of people without a nation. We must focus all on ONE nation, very organized, strictly, and gathering all together from all nations. And we need SPONSORS.

ONE rich, free, western-humanistic nation will be the jumpstart for ALL nations.

Because when ONE nation is revolutionized, the pallet example of this nation will change ALL other nations, as all citizens in all other nations will want our free healthcare system, and technological advancements in their own nations, having realized their current system purposefully discredited alternative science to diminish the population through e.g cancer.

And Norway is that nation. The nation which ALREADY has the world`s best social services and healthcare. A nation of former Vikings, and an enraged public that soon reaches boiling point. Or perhaps Norway has given up into the previously mentioned apathy.

And perhaps that apathy has developed into ¨I don`t give a damn, and would rather serve the system, and get paid. ¨ And just maybe that attitude of preprogramed apathy has led the Norwegian populace into Satanism, and the New World Order, abandoning their ethnicity, rights, culture, religion, and free healthcare just to seriously protect un-serious joker politicians, who would rather replace the human race. BUT I have not given up on my people...!!!

And if Norway won`t rebel, we have the fierce ENGLISH, or perhaps the FRENCH or ITALIANS?

England would be most suitable because: 1. English is the global language. 2 England once was the centre of the world during the Colonization Era. 3 And England fathered a previous technological revolution, namely the industrial revolution.

If the elite renegade scientists in England, like the ORC; combine their efforts with f.i the David Icke hype, and get some investigative journalist messiahs, a media-page, and unites the alternative world of anarchists, Anonymous, and New-Age, we might have a chance. IF we stay together. IF we focus mostly on ONE nation. But it all rests on YOU!

This nation (Norway) MUST undergo a reformation in all the branches of science, history, and our school-books be rewritten.

A technological revolution into the golden age of where the Sabbatean-Frankist-Jesuit-Illuminati are defeated by a glorious red army of the People like during the French revolution. The greatest moment in history.

The pivotal, historical moment when the people took back power, and created their OWN army with their OWN courts, and trialed the Sabbatean-Frankist-Jesuit-Illuminati to create an eternal, free, perpetual World Order.

As of now: The mighty freemasons own all the courts and lawyers. We need a rebellion. A revolution. A new constitution. And our OWN courts. But this cannot happen until the Army has grown in numbers, and have lawyers amongst our members.

Chapter 3: Hell or a golden age.

The Black Order, and their parasite state.

We have the privatization of TECHNOLOGICAL knowledge as our primary target as I will describe soon below.

We cannot observe the NWO conglomerate without noticing the elephant in the room which might, the Sabbatean-Frankist-Jesuit-Illuminati, but we will simply call them: The technocracy elite who see themselves as Gods ruling us the peasant slave-class. I call it a technocracy because that`s what it is. The experts in every field of school. The technological elite are basically black magicians ruled by the religious elite: The Illuminati, and the Vatican Jesuits, but we will not go there.

The dark state CIA, Area 51, and their transhumanism projects to make themselves ubermensch, and at the same time reduce us to monkeys.

THEY rattled the cage, and will have a parade of laughing monkeys, foxes, and alternative media before their parliament before they know it!

The NWO technocracy of secret societies, and their police sponsored by the super-rich, and led by the Satanic Illuminati Vatican Jesuits, sabbatean Jews, and royal Illuminati compromise:

1. The State we all know (education, police, hospital, social wellfare, military, government etc)
2. Monarchy
3. Secret Societies ruled by Monarchies (which must be banned – basically taken by force and exposed for sacrifice/Satanism etc)
4. Intelligence agencies (like the CIA`s Mk-Ultra),
5. Internationalist NWO organizations, and conglomerates like the Rockefeller foundation, the UN, and think-tanks like the Council on Foreign Relations etc.
6. Underground dark-state facilities, shadow-government, shadow-military DUMB`s, secret science facilities, – secret cities that the people`s army must take by force , and expose for the HORRIFIC crime of conspiring against all surface-dwellers, setting up what is basically a underground Satanic empire. We will expose their *SHADOW EMPIRE*.
7. Private capitalist mafias, e.g Illumicorporations, Rothschild banks and their assets, media, science-institutions and all corporations whose paid results/products/opinions are owned. These are the ones who keep evolution away from the people.
The science-intitutions, and firms will be our PRIMARY TARGET.

You can't win in court against banking-elites, corporations, the EU, or even secret Hollywood pedophilia. But when the people realize their RIGHTS for TECHNOLOGY through the best WELL-FARE-SYSTEM has been exploited, and kept secret for them for 90 years, they will rebel. 9/11 didn't wake them, but this will be it.

The technocracy use technology LIGHTYEARS ahead of us to clone, mind-control, and kill us. From where? Secret underground DEEP-STATE facilities. And there IS no deep state. It's not the real name for it. The real name is the DARK-STATE. For it is a DARK GLOBAL EMPIRE of Satanism, believe it or not, but we will make it a PEOPLE'S empire. Or perhaps a MONARCHY???

Crowning a King is the best solution for current monarchies!

Imagine if we had a King who represented the PEOPLE. Imagine if we won, and all remembered this King for a thousand generations. That is ONE good-old-traditional way for revolution, the old Alpha-Male Civilizer Sun-King Horus. They won't be able to shut THAT down, because nothing encourages people with pitchforks, (and teasing their pussies,) more than a super-idol King. (Which is basically what a King was back in the days, before the Hannovers took over, anyways.)

This might be a better route than going through the political arena, because *you simply cannot deny the people the right for a King.* And what's even better is that *all the King dictates is law.* So the pyramid will fall brick by brick whatever happens, IF you follow our commands, and raise up Messiahs.

The criminal record, and evidence for the Sabbatean-Frankist-Jesuit-Illuminati is ENORMOUS. The people only need to organize their king`s army, create their own king`s courts, and JUDGE them for THOUSANDS of crimes!!! Read the 25 goals of Weishaupt that got the Illuminati banned. It is the definition of crime.

Conspiracy to overthrow a nation-state is a CRIME punishable by DEATH in most countries! Show non-tolerance, and *anger whenever anyone brings up the* Illuminati *topic or sympathizes for them*.

They are antihuman activists! They just want to SHIT on everything, destroy the world down to 500.000.000, and remake it for themselves, with humanity as their slaves. They intend to rule us as Gods from outer space... Their royalty care only about themselves, and never represented the people. King Harald of Norway recently tweeted: ¨What shall we re-name Norway??? ¨

And nobody rebels... He is SHITTING on you. What gave him the right??? What more right does he have than you??? Is he not ¨less alpha male¨ than most Norwegian peers??? He is a NOBODY! He can`t even hold speeches, and much less hold the NATION together...!!! Isn`t it simply a racist disease of the past to be ruler by birth right, and to govern the parliament, AND the Freemasonic Lodge by birth right for such long periods??? Sounds like a spoiled, evil baby...!!!

I`m certain he feels like SHIT when going to bed! He probably shakes in his BOOTS before going out to the people at Independence Day! But when he comes back in, he`s probably laughing his royal ass off, just like all the corrupt politicians he OWN. Yes...

Did you not know that all European Kings are the leaders of each nation`s respective Freemasonic Lodge???

And why is he the king with the Lion`s crest? Because the Freemasons are Jews, and European royalty are descendants of (the historical) King David of Israel 3000 years ago.

So basic meltdown: An asshole from a bygone era claims racist supremacy to rule all in his nation, and you accept it??? This bygone, ancient tribe of Judah eats up thousands of formerly tribal European tribes, and you, as a Norwegian, let him get away with it!??

They`re racist criminals by definition! CRIMINAL CONSPIRATORS! What IS a King if not a conspirator??? Or ask yourself this: When was the last time the King represented the true will of the people...???

Listen to David Icke, and know that royals, or the royal arch of Freemasonry are the cornerstone of the ILLUMINATI.

They`re not the PEOPLE`s Kings... They are the ILLUMINATI KINGS, and their daughters are VAMPIRES and WHORES. And they are CERTAINLY not Christian, and will certainly not get away from their sinful betrayal!

The royals are WHORES of the Freemasonic lodge, the Jewish tribe of Judah, and the Rothschild dynasty that aim to destroy the world, and create a global, atheistic, Satanic, communistic dictatorship with a population of 500 million slaves!!! Because they claim superior right to rule you by BLOODLINE!

"Maintain humanity under 500.000.000" is chiselled in the Georgia Guidestones and is no secret.

Humanity is at war against the states, secret societies, and the monarchy. All have someone they loved who died of cancer. Even the police must REALIZE they cannot serve as crumbling rocks of the PYRAMID anymore! Dear policeman! Join us and seize these wolves in sheep`s clothing.

The world needs a new King... I recommend a Christian King Pope, who will be held to high standards. I recommend that the "King" is chosen by majority of votes by the Christians in the nation, and not by bloodline...

Read my book "The Kingdom of God. "

Having a King super-idol to symbolize the people, and our movement would be easiest, because you cannot denounce the will of the people to elect a new King or dethrone the old one. That is simply unhistorical... As humans are pack-animals inclined to Kingship or chieftainship by an alpha-male, deciding your own King is an instinctive right you cannot denounce, and if the people so choose, the King will be forced to abdicate by shame.

Or else we must do it ourselves. Like the French did during the French revolution. The People establishing their own army and courts.

If this revolution does not happen in a free, industrialized western country within 10-100 years: Humanity`s potential will be lost FOR-EVER, along with the green Earth, because once the Sabbatean-Frankist-Jesuit-Illuminati have control over the internet, TRUTH, ed-ucation, science, and the media, not to mention government, police, military and banks, they are not letting go.

The Illuminati WERE criminals, ARE criminals, and will FOREVER be remembered as criminals when the PEOPLE write THEIR his-tory-books on how THEY killed EVERYONE in 2 World Wars, with MILLIONS dying from cancer. When we create OUR schools with OUR truths, and every child is taught at school how THEY (the su-per-rich cabal) murdered billions!

It will be SO easy... Because God, the planet, and the stars are on our side. There is always hope, because hope is all we have. There-fore, there is ONLY hope. And We *will* win because We *must* win... The super-rich cabal have taken over the media, the culture, educa-tion, created false sciences, false history, taken over the banks, con-trol the financial world, and has control over politics. Our only option is to create cells, study groups, and families of light/knowledge. From there we will split up, grow new cell-groups, infiltrate society, recruit people from lawyers to biker-anarchists etc.

But we will start by investigative journalist`s provocative documentaries, and books aimed at the schools. Youth are very rebellious, pure, and open to new ideas that the elderly would NEVER believe. For what do we preach love and magical science???

Aim at the horny youth who easily become fascinated with our books, and program of revolution: Mysterious history, magical science of levitation, and eternal youth! Flying cars! Provoke the children, and the youth firstly because their hearts are pure, and their view of reality hasn`t solidified yet.

A child will cry when watching our documentaries on the SCOPE of Sabbatean-Frankist-Jesuit-Illuminati crime, and how many they killed. Provoke the children, and youth secondly because they are the foundation of tomorrow society, and the future doctors and scientists. The youth is the foundation. *Attack the foundation the pyramid will crumble brick by brick, even if it takes 50 years.* Because when 70% of the new generation are anti-nwo, society changes.

But what WILL deliver the final blow is investigative journalism.

Why work, serve and protect the state???

It is time to wake up. All you have been taught at school were lies. The technocracy *laugh at you!*

You are the biggest FOOL of all time, and a useless slave to reptilian overlords.

All the monsters were real. God, the devil, werewolves, vampires, reptilians and demons.
Your Hollywood movies portray a more realistic view of reality than what you`ve been taught at school.

All the fairytales were real... The giants before the flood, elves, ufo`s, levitating pyramid builders, and the ancient Annunaki kings ruled for 500.000 years uninterrupted only a few thousand years ago. You are food. Trash. The last 1000 years is the first age of Homo Sapiens Sapiens in 500.000 + years. I talked to American Indians, and there were giants in America until very recently. The "Gods" just went underground for nothing more than ONE second in 24 hours if intelligent life began 2 billion years ago, which I believe. Just to observe their little ants in their planetarium prison planet. Perhaps they would figure out this time, but no.

It`s time to realize you are a MERE HUMAN with NO VALUE to the system of bankers, and that nothing of what you heard from alleged prophets, and pastors of the round-earth lie were true. It was just a reflection of the super-conscience.

You are the GREATEST FOOL of ALL TIME, because you did not remember your history!
YOU ARE A WORTHLESS ASSET WITH NO TRIBE, NO ROOTS, NO BOOKS, NO SCIENTISTS, NO LEADERS, NO ILLUMINATI-FREE-NATION, NO TRUTH, NO HISTORY, NO RIGHTS, AND NO HUMAN INTELLIGENCE AGENCY!
Your irresponsibility will lead to another 500.000 years of Annunaki rule!
There`s not even a single Christian intelligence agency or government on the Earth! (The Vatican and Jehovah`s Witnesses are corrupt.) You have no NATION, no TRIBE, no RIGHTS and no leadership, escape-plan or government.
YOU`RE AN IRRESPONSIBLE IDIOT!!!

Why so serious when all you`ve ever been told at school are lies???
Why so serious about being angry when you KNOW the politicians lie. You KNOW it SO well, yet YOU are serious while THEY don`t give a DAMN about you...
Why so serious???

I don`t understand... Is it to protect them while they slowly kill the population down to 500.000.000??? IS IT!? Or is it not.

Either way, you`ll have to act instinctively as a non-compromise child as ALL have responsibility for their fellow humans, their nation, and the development of civilization.

Why so serious??? Have you not seen how they sacrifice ¨dull care¨ at the Satanic Bohemian Grove??? THEY_DON`T_CARE!!! It`s time you break down in laughter!

History was wrong, pretty much all of it, considering there were giants. Oh Thomas, that`s a sensitive issue, you might hurt someone`s feelings and impose your worldview on others!¨ So what! I try to help them because I care!

They seriously try to kill humanity, kill themselves, while you seriously try to protect them?!?

YOUR CIVILIZATION IS THE BIGGEST JOKE OF ALL CIVILIZA-
TIONS OF ALL TIME! There wasn`t even any resistance! You`re the
biggest joke since the Trojan horse!
It`s time you break down in laughter just like they do. They fooled
you! It`s a joke, a circus, and a game for souls!

Millions of policemen, doctors, and lawyers will join the People`s
Army when they realize their lives to seriously protect something as
un-serious as the lying Illuminati politicians serves no purpose than
simply killing, and sacrificing the population for their souls, their
money, and for war, as they express in their Satanic rituals.

The People`s Army are the watchers watching the watchers, and the
REAL protectors of the people now that the police, and government
serve foreign, monetary, secret-society, and even outright satanic
factions!

They serve the government, and secret societies who pay them, and
not the taxpayers who pay for the government! It`s all corrupt!

They conduct BRUTAL experiments on the human population, and
are blind to real problems like rape, and drug-traffic which the secret
police secretly PROMOTE!

Ok, let me get this straight... The secret police have gay-clubs,
drugs, and child-porn, so they ally with the OTO, and hire the politicians... Then they BRIBE you, policemen, with this. In this way one
could say that they protect you, and you protect them, as you are all
accomplices in the most-grave crimes... ... ... And then the police
in Kristiansand sold their child-porn (me) to the Churches, and the
biker-gangs... (... ...) Then they ALL became policemen, right?

We need a revolution, boys! And we must act soon, and in a western civilized nation before they impeach free speech, and the free
internet. Even beautiful young singers, and aspiring scientists like
myself are brutally cloned and murdered. Yet I have chosen to for-
give.

Because divine, unconditional, endless, merciful love completely shatters, and destroys hate and darkness.

Will you let their Hell be YOUR Hell!?!

The elderly generations are rootless generations of post-American slaves without identity or religion, serving as food for THEIR Hell.

Will you let THEIR Hell be YOUR Hell??? Or will you be a victorious child, growing up to be the first father-generation in 100 generations? The first generation gifted knowledge.

From what we`ve learnt so far, it`s due time you start questioning the your most solid ideas of reality.
And what is this reality? Go read David Icke!

Because our NWO is a soul-tax-farm, and nothing else. We are OVER-RUN by fallen angels/higher-dimensional beings of greater power than ourselves, who were defeated a long time ago, (at the end of the last ice-age), but are coming back
We live in the timeframe of a SECOND between intelligent life on Earth, a wide variety of ¨alien humanoids,¨ be them giants, platinum blonde angels or reptilians.
These reptilians are most probably a species that evolved in the Jurassic era, popularly called Seraphim in the Bible, like the Swedish Seraphim Order, as they are regarded as a species of angels in Judaism.
Popularized as an incredibly capable and intelligent humanoid race, it is likely they populated Earth for a very long time, perhaps extremely long time, with many both ascending and descending.

Yes, we have been invaded. Some call them demons, others call them reptilian aliens, but the old scaretales of heroes fighting dragons are certainly real. And YOU`RE IN IT!

They have even come so far they have created artificial intelligence, and uploaded every mind into a supercomputer to control all souls, emotions and responses. It's the wet dream of reptilian, masonic scientists. The younger generation grew up with the Matrix.

Any resistance is killed off by electronic harassment, and voodoo from this self-aware, artificially intelligent, satellite (they are actually UFO`S) based embodiment of the demonic hierarchy, with threats of losing your health, your mental health, losing your jobs, and being completely isolated from the irresponsible, apathetic pseudo-Christian elder generation. The elder generations are bribed with money and philosophy, believing the lies of evolution, physics, history, religion, etc. The younger generation is bribed off with sex, real-life hunger-games, technology, and secret knowledge.

The intelligence creating the Matrix is a perfect, holy, loving, forgiving humanoid intelligence. Whatsoever energy that cannot be recycled is deleted. This is the dire, most important truth mankind can embrace at the moment.

There is more at stake than just race, language, history, borders, rights and politicians. This is about the survival of humanity against artificially reconstructed races of ancient reptilians, who are back, and wants the world for themselves. (Of course. I mean. What did you expect? That they would just sit there, serve us, or become Christian humanists???) This world is VERY, VERY old. It's so old and full of mysteries that it's time we start a People`s Army paranormal research group, to find the truth about Hell, the afterlife, Heaven, it`s entries, and broadcast our discoveries to all mankind united.

It is therefore time with a People`s Army that unites all ethnicities, religions, and cultures for the greatest war the world has ever seen! The war for the survival of humanity.

A golden age of enlightenment?

Universal enlightened brotherhood through common ethics is the only way to keep the world secure. WHEN we reach disclosure on technology: Electricity will be so cheap, cars will run on water, and healthcare will be so cheap: We will DEFINITLY end up with a socialist state with a futuristic social welfare system that will spread like fire to all nations because of advanced technology in hospital automatization.

We will create the world's first ILLUMINATI-FREE NATION! But perhaps start with a village, school, renting a conference-room, or taking our children to summer-youth-camps???

It will be FANTASTIC BEYOND WORDS! Free healthcare. Zero death. Fusion powerplants. Water-hydrogen powerplants! Antigravity propulsion transport and architecture. Hydrogen-water powered cars. CARS running on WATER! Antigravity/levity cars! Yes, I know people who can make all these dreams come true...

I have ALOT of scientists on my team. Join the New World Community online!!!

What the world NEEDS today is for ONE pioneering industrialized nation (Norway or France would be perfect) to undergo a revolution into the golden age of technology where the Sabbatean-Frankist-Jesuit-Illuminati is defeated. Because when ONE light is lit, the whole world lights up! The first ILLUMINATI-FREE NATION!

Whon our police, hospitals, and elected officials no longer serve the people who elected them, but serve foreign capital interest affairs of the Satanic Illuminati, what must inevitably happen?

Like during the French revolution. Where the people take back power, and create their OWN army with their OWN courts and trial:

1 The Sabbatean-Frankist-Jesuit-Illuminati Monetary Elite. (Satanic capitalists)

2 The Sabbatean-Frankist-Jesuit-Illuminati Cultural Elite. (The Satanic Illusionists)

3 The Sabbatean-Frankist-Jesuit-Illuminati Technocratic Elite. (The Satanic doctors, scientists and teachers)

And more.

Exposing the latter will be the goal of this revolution. The New Earth Community will replace the quackademics of science, medicine, physics and history. ALL must be replaced. That is the goal of this revolution.

Read the 25 goals of Weishaupt and know that conspiracy to over-throw a nation-state is a CRIME! They are CRIMINALS!

They have inverted reality, but I`m here to wake you up!

YOUR reality is fictional. Conspiracy IS reality.

WE the PEOPLE decide reality: When we have the books, the sci-ence - the schools. The VILLAGE! (Or youth-camp.)

The people are taking back the power from the Sabbatean-Frankist-Jesuit-Illuminati!!!

I remember when I saw Dan Brown`s Angels and Demons. I didn`t know about the Illuminati at that time, and they frightened me…

The Illuminati are back!?!?!? WAKE UP!

We DEFEATED them once before.

Now we will CRUSH them with LAUGHTER!

And when all know their CRIMES of the last 4 centuries: The world will HATE the Illuminati, and fear conspiracy SOO much, they will NEVER rise again, and mankind will be free, united, and happy for-ever!

THEY shall lose their HEAD! Whence we have the people and proof. MY head MUST remain on my shoulders where it belongs.

Love must replace pride, or the west will die.

There is only one way to get revolution, and I will explain it to you. The 20ies, 30ies, 40ies, 50ies, 60ies, and 70ies had their rebellion for feminism, equality, black rights etc. That was their ZEITGEIST which is German for "timespirit." And today: All we have is LGBT pride parades! The millennial lifestyle is happily ignorant with Iphones, Tv`s, and life in a post-modern Hollywood culture. The current zeitgeist should however be a RENAISSANCE of technology, rights and information. We either chose an age of intellect where the people overcome the technocracy, or we chose an age of slavery, and class society.

Our elected officials answer to foreign, and globalist monetary powers, and that is a fact, not a conspiracy. Our Norwegian prime minister Erna Solberg, and Crown Prince Haakon attend the secret, elitist Bilderberg meetings where the elite discuss behind closed doors. That is the DEFINITION of conspiracy. So, we are in no way lunatics.

Our show is led by three main elites, all of whom are associated with the Sabbatean-Frankist-Jesuit-Illuminati NWO conspiracy goal and have no moralistic ideals aside "survival of the fittest. " These groups are the

1. Globalist monetary (capitalist) elite whom demands ass-licking, and bribe world governments with money, power, sex and drugs.
2. The cultural elite brainwashing the people into ignorance.
3. The technocratic elite which are the technological elite of doctors, lawyers, policemen, all whom are experts, and leaders in their respective field of science, selling lies about which cure is the best for cancer. The fields of health education, and the elite health officials will be our main target. Nr. 3…

These three groups are non-national, and answer to their global, Satanic secret society: The Sabbatean-Frankist-Jesuit-Illuminati. It is true that many involved in these 3 elite groups are Nazis, and also Jews, but that is only their mask under which evil can operate. Their morale is "divide and conquer", "mankind is inclined to evil, not good", "order through chaos", "make, and keep people sick to earn money from drugs", "evil is good" and "survival of the fittest" etc. Or as George Orwell wrote in his 1984 book: "Freedom is slavery, ignorance is strength, and war is peace." The Illuminati are Satanists, and the Satanic ideology is all about inverting truth.

That is why they create a false reality, a false history, false science, false education, and give us terrible MEDIEVAL healthcare. Their masonic goals can be found on the Georgia Guidestones where it is written in 12 languages: Maintain humanity`s population under 500.000.000. Since they worship power, they are all control freak megalomaniacs, and want to create a world of perpetual slavery, and darkness for our mind, bodies and souls.

As money rules the 21st century world, and Judeo-Christian morale dies out with the elderly, the old morale of kindness, love, compassion, meekness, servitude, lowliness, charity, respect, equality, and that all have innate human value has been replaced by: Job, career, money, how much sex you have, power, pride, greed, and even betrayal is now regarded as "good morale" because it shows you are strong, as "survival of the fittest/most evil." It has become "cool" to be a criminal, murdering Illuminati agent, and "cool" to be a badboy.

The happy, loving, compassionate moralistic Christian flower-kid (like myself) is seen as inadequate, weak, and not suited for work. This infuriates me. The Illuminati is CRIMINAL by all standards after its 25 criminal goals and CANNOT be compromised in any way.

The west is losing its humanistic foundation of morale. Without it: The west will not survive. All high-cultures, and high-civilizations accomplished great deeds only because these people had a homogenous culture/ethics/morale as Aristotle argues. Immigration, and _poor integration_ of Muslims have caused a rape epidemic, a terror epidemic, a crime epidemic, and a decrease in work. Most immigrants live on welfare, and that is a fact. They have flooded our prisons, taken our taxes to welfare, and if they never had come here: _Scandinavia would INEVITABLY had undergone an economic, industrial, technologic, cultural, and national-romantic renaissance into a high-civilization with a strong sense of unity among the population, and with zero crime rates._

But the problem isn`t immigrants, but our paid corrupt politicians and their Sabbatean-Frankist-Jesuit-Illuminati war-brokers who CREATE wars, resulting in poor immigrants.
And the main problem is not Islam, but cultural Marxist politicians who betrayed their nation, corrupt national and international leaders.

The result is a society of a hundred sub-culture groups, whereas we would have been ONE dominating culture had it not been for immigration. 100`s of subcultures live in fear, and hate against each other, but under ONE flag. The result is a population losing it`s power because they are divided among themselves, while the state becomes a police-state, and gains MORE power since the people crave more protection from violence, rape, terror, and crime caused non-integrated immigrants.

There is no longer a people`s state since there is no people anymore, and the state thus becomes an cancer feeding to preserve its own powerful existence, because it`s ruled by power-hungry men and women. The state becomes a hive for power-hungry career politicians, and becomes based on power, and competition, not unity. Because there is no common humanistic ethic in the population.

We must preserve western humanism, or the west will fall like any other historical high civilization, as Aristotle argues... The Satanic morale of pride, money, power, sex, envy, crime, and betrayal must be replaced by love, equality, compassion, or what I like to call ¨the Judeo-Christian western heritage.¨

This can come through a ¨reloveution hippie anti-Illuminati zeitgeist¨, or a ¨national-romantic renaissance rebellion. ¨ But these are however unlikely. The only realistic revival of western humanistic values is through uniting both immigrants, and nationalists in the fight for freedom of rights to better healthcare, whereupon mankind will be free from their illusions as the Satanic cabal falls.

If one card falls (the medicinal technocracy) , the entire Sabbatean-Frankist-Jesuit-Illuminati house of cards will tumble, and humanity will have a new zeitgeist of outspoken hatred against the lies of the Satanic elite. Everyone will realize their Illuminati governments have lied to them, and true history will be written, and the Illuminati will never rise again because our children will hate them from reading true history schoolbooks. That is our ONLY realistic hope against a NWO. Imaginary religious hopes in for instance Jesus` Second Coming is playing right into the NWO`s hands as it is a waste of time, and energy that could otherwise have been used for humanity as a whole, like this investigative journalist technological revolution-evolution into a New-Age.

Do you not see how dangerous this social experiment is? With 100`s of subcultures, ethnic, and religious groups. With borders vanishing, and a *post-Hollywood global culture emerging perhaps 100 years from now, we* are not more far away from a global NWO communist dictatorship by these power-hungry three elites: 1 Monetary, 2 Cultural, 3 and Technocrat. Which is their aim. Because: They`re addicted to power and control.

Create a inter-religion/ethic of TRUE science!

But if knowledge is power, and science is knowledge, science must therefore determine if God exists! How can God be truth and science too at the same time if they oppose each other? Because science is quackademia. To unite the people against the technocracy`s power through knowledge, we first need a new, true, scientific religion.

Religion has always been the core of society as the unifying factor of any society as representing the moralistic backbone, but was always combined with sacred science, which we often forget.

Any true civilization has had sacred science as it`s backbone, now monopolized by the Freemasons. All ancient civilizations expressed their sacred science in the geometry, and symbolism of architecture. Phi, the Flower of Life, sacred geometry, and sacred astrology, which was sacred knowledge of the divine Creator that humbled humanity and made these civilizations strong and united, capable of creating such architectural marvels. A post-modern society in which religion doesn`t represent sacred science, and unifies all people is NOT A CIVILIZATION, but medieval sheep with Iphones indoctrinated by Hollywood. We never graduated from medieval alchemy. That`s when quackademia took over with Newton and Galileo Galilei.

We now live in a post-civilization, post-humanist, multicultural, cultural-Marxist, post-American, ego, and satisfaction culture. Pride, beauty, muscles, money, sex, betrayal, and power are the core values of not only the west, but the entire world and have replaced the Christian core values upon which all western civilization was founded, morale, respect, honesty, meekness, piety, lowliness, humbleness, politeness, kind-heartedness, love, forgiveness, and the humanistic treaty on equality: That all men are born equal with rights.

In what way are we equal if there is no God who defines our worth? In what way are we equal if not for the everlasting soul that ascends or descends? Without these two eternal factors: God and Soul, mankind is no better than an animal, and the result is a cold society of selfishness where dog eats dog. Humans scavenging their own race trying to earn more money instead of cooperating to build monuments of civilization like the ancients did in unity.

Why? Because we do not have the sacred science of religion upon which the ancient world was founded. I am speaking of sacred geometry, the knowledge of God/Gods, the ether, the spiritual, the eternal soul, and the multiverse.

A system where physics, and education was inseparable from sacredness, and religion, as was in Egypt up through all history until the Satanic Illuminati invented their FALSE physics, false theory of evolution, etc, to propagate "survival of the fittest", and most importantly: Erase mankind's spiritual nature, and knowledge about the spiritual/ether completely.

Ether. The Greek name for the most important of all the five elements. Civilization started with Sumer, ancient India, and primarily Egypt and Phoenicia from which sprung ancient Canaan, Israel, Christianity, and also the Greek civilization. Yet all these had common that priesthood, and education was inseparable, for they had the key upon which all civilization was founded. Sacred knowledge about physics...

Sacred science, which they expressed through geometry in architecture. Science we have forgotten. We are not a civilization but cattle, if we are to be objective, historical, and compare ourselves to the ancient philosopher athletes upon which our civilization was founded. That is why we need a reformation unity revival into a global, reformed Mother Church, and a technological revolution renaissance to incorporate sacred principles of science of spirit, and sacred illegal physics into our religion, and a revival of national romance. And we need it today.

The Reformation Revival Revolution Renaissance of Love and Light

We need a reformation revival revolution renaissance in in all sciences, and levels of society today - because a safe foundation for a future warm society can only come through ethical unity, not ethnical unity, based on universal truths proven by science - the language of today!

Peace cannot be obtained by the mixing ethnicities, or mixing cultures into a "global America."

Peace can only come through ethical unity. Something all ethnicities, and religions can agree upon! Which is humanism, the humanistic values, and the humanistic, scientific inter-religious religion love and light.

New-Age science, and TRUE science of the spiritual contradicts modern "science" which is not science at all, but masonic propaganda to inhibit the evolution of truth, and the reality of the ETHER: The spiritual aspect of physics.

Modern science contradicts Wilhelm Reich, and Niclola Tesla, is not science at all, and has become a "scientific *religion of quackademics*", which you will find evidence for in my videos. Our school curriculum are not "theories", but wrong hypothesis *created by the FREEMASONS which there is evidence for.*

Religion is only belief, and since science is just a stupid masonic religion, both science, and regular religion must reform.

As religion, and science historically walked hand in hand, and was inseparable from Egypt up to the Renaissance, how come religion avoids undergoing the scientific method of thesis-antithesis? If religion is not scientifically true, then if must of course be put to rest!

Yes. A purpose of our revolution is that ALL RELIGION must undergo the scientific method of thesis-antithesis, fall as either lies or superstition, or be rendered to science. How come we let medieval, fascist, political, and judicial systems survive in the 21st century?

How come ALL scholarly fields undergo scientific validity-tests ASIDE from the most important one: Religion. Religion which has caused so much blood. All religion must undergo a scientific, philosophical, and humanistic validation test to either stand, or be discarded.

And the remaining ethics still standing, provable by Science, which is my religion of Source, Love and Light, but also Tantric Buddhism, Buddhism, my own Nazarene (www.1stcenturyministries.com) Christianity, Comparative Mythology, Animism, Shamanism, Astrology and Zuism, for instance, will be the New-Age spiritual backbone of a new world of new physics: To bridge the gap between the sheeple and the MASONIC version of history, science, and create a TRUE CURRICULUM for future generations of children!

Every person is responsible for his brother and changing the world. Why??? Everyone has the possibility to do so through the internet. Nothing is impossible. Everything is possible.

YOU can create a world SO fantastic...! Everything you ever dreamt of… Levitation… Eternal life… You MUST!

Forge an IDEA so GOOD that it`s very inception makes it completion inevitable. For there are ONLY possibilities, because there is always hope, and because hope is all we have, there is ONLY hope. Always.

What we see is that New-Age is fore-running Christianity in spiritual evolution, conspiracy theory, and exposing the Satanic Illuminati dark state, CIA Mk-Ultra, globalism, Jewry, inside jobs, and state-cover-up of true etheric science, spirit-science, and technology that could save the world if exposed.

Which when exposed is the key to awaken the masses, because people are so gullible today that they won`t rebel against the Satanic Illuminati unless they understand they've been robbed from the cure to cancer.

When studying alternative history, the ether, physics, and medicine you will discover that most resources you find up-to-date with the

21st century evolution of mankind, can be categorized as in the "New-Age Movement", while my writings would be considered "New-Age Christianity."

New-Age today means you believe there might be a God or Goddess, several Gods, good, and bad aliens, conspiracy-reality, and certainly a spiritual reality. Perhaps that is where we also belong, but we are a People's Army for everyone, as long as they are true to the humanistic rights..

Most Christians are asleep. Believe me...! I tried EVERYTHING. Even knowing that the Satanic Illuminati is behind wars, financial depression, financial tyranny/terrorism, and 9/11 didn't awaken them. But when they realize grandma could have been cured from cancer, they will, of course, REBEL. And rebel BIG TIME.

Chapter 4: The People`s Army`s First Free Federation (FFF).

I tried for a whole month, but I *seriously* could not come up with a better term for our United Conspiracy Theorist`s Global Movement than the FFF, although it`s the 6th letter of the alphabet. Our end-goal is (of course) to create the first Illuminati free nation through disclosing TRUTH to the public, criminalizing, and ridiculing other nations antihuman projects, like chemtrails and propaganda to hide it. A federation is a collection of common interests, like f.i a trade federation.

We call ourselves ¨The People`s army.¨

We are a federation of all enterprises with our common aim. A nation without borders. We are a humoristic, humanist, inter-political, inter-religious, multi-ethnic movement of *INVESTIGATIVE JOURNALISTS* fighting in the great meme-wars. Training to become one, and wake people up is your current mission.
We are revolutionaries, scholars, and reform scientists which does not mix religion with politics, and want to:
1. Give cheaper, and more efficient medical care through promoting technological advancements to the people through investigative journalist disclosure of a global medical conspiracy that affects billions of lives and will threaten trillions, e.g secret cancer cures.
2. Preserve western human bio-diversity, humanism, and human rights against any form of state or ideology.

We have love, light, and laughter (compassion, enlightenment and humour) as motto, and we SHOULD be a humoristic-humanitarian banner under which all ethnic groups, and all religions are united through the inter-religious law of Source, Love and Light, as in my book: The Scientific Religion of the Sun.

We SHOULD have the red, and black flag of social-anarchy/anarcho-syndicalism as our flag, which is displayed on the cover of this book.

Why so serious? All your life is after all based on lies fabricated by Jokers. It`s time we realized we`ve been fooled, put on the mask, and start making fools of them instead!

Our Goals?

All our primary goals can be summed up in reformation revival revolution renaissance. The 4 R`s.

Our first goal is rewriting sciences for a reformation in education, universities, and science through rewriting physics, history, and medicine which currently are based on masonic lies for those who researched Nicola Tesla, Wilhelm Reich, Royal Raymond Reiss, and a DOZEN others including for instance Thomas Joseph Brown, and investigative expert David Wilcock. Just to name a few popular to get the ball rolling.
This must be done in our very secretive beginnings, by hoarding books, authors, and experts from field of science, and every branch of society to our cause. Before the next goal.

Our secondary goal is disclosure of technology through hardcore investigative journalism, and political demands through peaceful parades of idiotic display of their crimes. Art, comedy-plays, memes, and revolutionary music. We will break all the norms of politics, race, sex and correctness like a wild, humorous bunch of anarchist socialist savages.

Going forth with humour is something all can relate to, which will spread like wildfire, and make everyone join the parade, because it`s just as crazy, and somewhat hilarious what our politicians have been doing, if seen from the right view.
Our third goal would be to create an Ubuntu economy.

As the Satanic media prime role is to weaken the human spirit through seriousness, focusing on war, suffering, and how the state is there for your protection, the media will simply collapse, as their entire system fails, and doctors, policemen, politicians, and the media will have to answer a laughing nation of sexual savages standing at the gates of parliament demanding answers to chemtrails and "is all physics wrong" Lol.

When they say yes, because they can`t say no, we will simply be EVEN more harsh, and never give up until we take over the media and make official broadcastings on the crimes, conspiracies, cures, and the People`s Army`s People`s Courts has condemned these political Jokers to public hanging, done to the cheer of a million protesters.

As long as you have love, light, lust and laughter as motto, I guarantee you the police will stand down and let you straight into the parliament, preventing martial law as there is nothing for the police to gain on defending the conspiracy, as they were only bribed with sex and drugs, and the People`s Army alternative is better.

And the INFOWARRIORS must strike NOW before they strike US with viruses, nuclear-war, food shortage, steal our economy, or shut down our internet.

Expose them through investigative disclosure, and massive broadcasting on all internet platforms.

Our motto is Love, Light, Lust and Laughter.

Our battle-cries are:

People have the right of a state where politicians serve the people of the nation, not monetary conglomerates and foreign interest think tanks. A state that gives them the best available healthcare, education and technology. A state that cares, not lies.

And start from there.

Why so serious???

We will awaken every single person in all the world, and we will do it through playing on conspiracies with comedy, branding our elected officials as traitorous jokers to be laughed at before the gallows.

The Purpose of a People`s Army?

Our aim as the people`s army is to protect, and represent the people, and not a political opinion. This is the People`s Army. It`s not about white vs black, Islam vs Christianity, or left vs right politics. We are the watchers watching the watchers. When the state has become a parasite vampirizing the people for it`s own existence, we need a revolution to give power back to the people. When the state no longer represents the people, but serve money, capitalism, and secret societies interests: It is time the people create an army that serves the people and watch the watchers. Watching the state`s media-propaganda and crimes, protecting the people from the state. The army of the people is dedicated at doing the job of what the state SHOULD have done.

Our aim is to keep world peace for as long as possible! You can hold a balloon under-water by force, but once you let go, everything reverts back to normal. We reach ascension as a species. Global enlightened brotherhood through free internet information. It is just a matter of time, unless they start a war to put us against each other. No communist police-state world order! We the people will create the NWO on our own! Don`t go against the political zeitgeist! Use globalism and socialism against them! Drop everything you have, focus on creating global ideas of peace, love, light, lust and humanism, because if they start a war, we revert back to the 60ies.

The People`s enemies will be judged once the People`s Army establish the People`s Courts – like during the French revolution.

We will thus PUSH forth all technological, socialist, and medical advancements in the ONE nation (like Britain or Norway) ALL of the FFF focused on. Because when the People have superior technology in ONE nation: All others will HAVE to change in conformity as the media simply collapses due to the widespread internet.

When humanity has ONE light, the entire room is lit, and ALL revealed. ALL members of the worldwide FFFederation must focus ALL on lighting that ONE candle for the world…
If we cannot get this nation, we will have to start a peaceful community to protect ourselves from the parasite state which suffocates us and eats our lives and money.

Such a community can in itself be the LIGHT the world needs to spark technological revolution renaissance globally: If we are clever activists, and use media, and the internet correctly. But we need SCIENTISTS, and doctors from all schools of society.

I myself a patron for the Free Thought Project, the Anonymous Movement, the secret ORC (which needs a mediaplatform) and the New Earth Community. Those are the organization I recommend cooperating with in the FFF.

Our third goal is for the New Earth Community, and the ORC to create ENLIGHTENED PHILOSOPHER KING`S, who are ALTERNATIVE SCIENTISTS (ether scientists) , INVESTIGATIVE JOURNALISTS, TALENTED SPEAKERS, HUMOROUS ACTORS, and TALENTED SINGERS to become SUPER-STAR MESSIAHS to breakthrough a technological reformation/revolution in a western-humanistic, free, industrialized country. Something they can`t shut down. (We`ll just use parades and play on music, dance and sexuality.)

We will infiltrate, and reform.
1. The media. (Internet meme-wars, article-writing, YouTube, alternative media)
2. Education. (Schools, universities: Science in general: History included)
3. Politics. (Both left and right) We will make protests with torches. (Lightbearer)
4. The financial sector. (Marketing, clothe-codes, tech-products, medicine, enterprise, think-tanks etc)

We cannot expect to win ONLY through involvement in the political arena, but will of course influence, and put PRESSURE on them as well through infiltrating and uniting humanist patriots of different parties.

Every member gets a USB pen with info on hidden tech, and info on the conspiracy to hide knowledge. The knowledge I will show, and YOU make public!

Our stance on Religion?

Our stance on religion is that we are officially etheric scientists and humanists. We believe in the will, and the power of good inherent in mankind, who I believe IS inherently good, contrary to Illuminati belief who teach we are all evil.

We believe in compassion, and a warm society. I personally believe in Source, Love, and Light as the scientific religion of humanism, but that is just me personally. Yet do you have a better solution???

It`s the only option I had as of now, although I deep-down have a sliiight belief Jesus will come on a wonderous white horse, and subdue all evil people, including other etherical shapeshifters, from this horse. Must be one incredible horse!

No, I`m just kidding, Jesus second coming was a Mazzaroth, and Pyramidal prophecy that was originally meant for Lucifer, architect of the Great Pyramid, and not Jesus at all.

It`s a scam used to control EVERY generation. "The fact that the world is evil just means Jesus is coming soon! "

Bullshit. There will always be an antichrist.

Yet most of the world today are religiously confined to absolute doctrines from medieval books.

How can we let the elephant in the room escape the scientific method? RELIGIO. Supremacism. The cause of ALL modern war, and ALL western social upheaval? Abrahamic religion is nothing but a ghost from the past. A TERRIFYING force of evil used to enslave people for millennia.

The revolution campaign for a peaceful NWO for the west craves heroism. It is accomplished by societal groups, not lonely individuals, but societal groups uniting that have the same program outlined in this book…

Will your religious group wilfully reform from to benefit our true cause? Please contact me. Our religious movement/revolution would create perpetual peace. Those called include political parties, think-tanks, philosophers, human-etic foundations, well-fare-organizations, etc, as well as religious establishments, IF they are willing to resort to the reason of the scientific method and REFORM.

The worldwide pallet for peace:

1 Revolutionary love is the only immortal, global culture that can save, and unite the world for perpetual balance, coherent in all humans. Traversing all borders and ethnicities.

The code for this eternal law is Love and Light. Love is akin to the word Law. Love is morale, respect, kindness, heart etc. Light is truth, enlightenment, expression, brain and deliverance. Heart, and mind distinguish us from animals, as chimpanzees scientifically has no human intellect, or concept of self-sacrifice. Combine them, and you create morale.

Animals are purely egocentric contrary to humans whom COMBINE mind/light, and love/heart to produce: MORALE!!! And what morale is there except love and light?

Both love, and light are Life. Without these two, nothing life would exist. They are the scientific creator, the circle of Life. Light and love is the eternal lesson for humanity to cultivate. Therefore;

2 God is love and light. How come that all sciences of the 21st century advance as they undergo the scientific method of thesis-antithesis except religion – which was science to our ancestors up until only 400 years ago? Away with idiotic tolerance and relativism! You could not learn to read unless you became a priest only 300 years ago! Science and religion was inseparable, but now it`s othwerwise?!

Therefore, enlightenment must render religion reduced to science, and cannot escape the scientific method under an investigative People's Army effort, and a university of all religions craved established. They will discover that through the etheric science, the science of comparative religion, and doctorates on religion (which I studied intensively) that;

3 The God of all Abrahamic religions is the same both from a linguistic, historical, and spiritual perspective. (To which I can testify greatly) And God is just a concept of pantheism united in a single conscience. AND that religion boils down to ancient myth, superstition and astrology popularly called astrotheology. Medieval myths, and anti-human, anti-liberal laws of enslavement cannot be tolerated in the 21st century if science has spoken against them!!! As religion has been the cause, and is the cause of especially all CURRENT wars, therefore;

4 Since the Abrahamic God is the same both in name, and since God is merely a concept, now defined through etheric science as the ALL, all ARE all the children of God, thus equals, and we crave an END to idiotic religious war, and the right of claiming his/hers religion is superior to others through criminalizing anything but the scientifically, historically, and spiritually true religion.

Institutionalized supremacist fascist religion – especially when mixed with politics - has a bloody trail through history, and must end, and be replaced with Source, Love and Light. We thus crave the University of Spiritual Science to establish a judicial court against all claim of false religious/spiritual superiority, and claim of religious sole truths with non-compromise to other truths, criminalizing all organized supremacist religions that are non-confirmative with free will, etheric science, human evolution, human liberty, and freedom of expression – criminalizing their institutions –criminalizing all violations against modernization of liberty, law, and UN human rights. *Or simply: Common 21st century human sense.*

All state religion must be criminalized unless modernized by the People's Army Declaration of Human Rights, and the scientific religion of Source, Love and Light.

Christianity reformed long ago and is very compatible with the scientific religion of love and light, and atheistic humanism. It poses no threat to freedom of expression, and liberty whatsoever.

And must be criminalized, as is common sense…

Sorry to take your religion away from you. Read my books on the subject.

Chapter 5: How to create the needed revolution.

You are dying (if you didn`t know)!

A hypothetical revolution in the west must be about knowledge is power, power-to-the-people, civil-rights to be heard, and about humanism. About love and light = compassion and enlightenment/knowledge. Compassion e.g in the form of social welfare. Reforming the medical industry and saving billions of cancer patients.

America has a great platform for New-Age, conspiracy theorists, and alternative scientists whereas Norway has close to none. We must start Families of (love and) Light/Knowledge, or Cell Groups where we study conspiracy reality, the crimes of the elite, and the hidden technology before we unleash a co-ordinated investigative journalism campaign with the aim of bringing down the government through exposing their LIES and marching on the parliament and media.
Information for disclosure is VITAL since the people will never revolt unless they are starving or lose their liberty. We must make them REALIZE that although they give you Iphones, Ipads, movies, and computers to create that "illusion of happiness", we are in fact DYING. Not only are millions dying from lack of proper healthcare like chemotherapy cancer treatment -

(*due to the Rockefeller family that funded the America health-organization (FDA), and started the Norwegian health-organization (NHI). Rockefeller who has had connections to the* Sabbatean-Frankist-Jesuit-Illuminati *since the beginning.*)

They are destroying us through vaccines, toxic additives in food, gmo, pesticides, chlorine in water (that calcifies the pineal gland), and poisoning us through chemtrails.
Chemicals like Aspartame works to destroy the DNA and will lead to the future population being born with both physical deformities, and mental disorders certain studies show.

Over time, the Kalergi plan aims to create a ¨negroid European race¨ while other Sabbatean-Frankist-Jesuit-Illuminati members call for the creation of a ¨European slave-race with an average IQ of about 90 – just clever enough to perform work. ¨

With the media slaughtering all right-wing activists, and traditional conspiracy theorists, the only hope for humanity is a technological, and socialist revolution of love, creating a utopian future welfare system.

Revolutionary possibilities.

The world needs revolution, and it can come through 1 Sexual Revolution, 2 Nationalist Revolution, 3 Religious Revolution, 4 Technological Revolution, 5 Political Revolution - dissatisfaction with lying politicians which ties with all of the above. People, including myself have tried all of the above for centuries to little effect, aside from number 4, technological revolution.

But what better motto than to combine the sexual revolution of Lady Liberty`s ¨we want freedom¨ with that of technology, enlightenment and Love?
Love, Light, Lust and Laughter of the Revolution Renaissance!
(Which happens to be our scientific, humanistic inter-religious religion, and the metaphysical concept of God.) Read my book.

We need sexy, famous, pussy-power superstar jokers without fear, to tare through to mainstream media through explicit parades, and bring news of the technological revolution to the masses at any cost! Such figures that the fan scores would see as ¨messiahs.¨
Both cultural messiahs (superstars) , media-messiahs (teachers) , and political messiahs (chieftains) are needed for our success.

Without leaders that are both humorous, cultural, and political such as this: It would be hard to cheer up, and activate our citizens who have become gullible, apathic sheep:

¨Oh! She died of cancer! ¨ / Watches Hollywood movies 1hr later while laughing, and preoccupied on the phone. Never thinking of investigating alternative cancer cures…

How many million times has such a scenario happened before someone needs to wake up the masses???

This makes me furious, personally.

The people WILL arise! Do you think it will be hard? Once exposed, and once a thousand citizens show their asses physically to the Prime Minister with humorous slogans, they, and their ¨oh so serious ¨ media will feel SO ashamed of their lies, as their proud, politically correct, serious character is only laughed at, and made fun of, reducing their character so thin as the piece of paper which says he/she is the prime-minister. They won`t be taken seriously anymore, and we would have won.

Basically… This is not only a necessity, but a responsibility for future generations that I want to be FUN and EASY!

Free healthcare. Zero death. Fusion powerplants. Local or personal water-hydrogen powerplants (as in the Tesla village of Croatia, or our Mauritius project with brother Tomislav Tesla.)

Domestic and personal antigravity propulsion transport and architecture. All you can DREAM of! Water-hydrogen electrolysis powered cars. CARS running on WATER! A utopia where nobody starves, suffer illness, and poverty is forgotten. EASY within reach for the first time in world history.

But before you start jumping into futuristic-new-age, and alternative science, we need to start a revolution, and boy will it be FUN! Boy, we will look back at what we accomplished and how it was SO EASY. The progress of the 21st century invites you to plant an idea so good that its inception makes its completion inevitable! Utopia! We just need enough enlightened youth. YOU are now a part of it, and must dedicate all your time, and effort to it. People used to believe in right and wrong.

Memento mori. Remember death. Today`s generation try to forget death with immediate satisfaction shortcuts to happiness, but our ancestors lived short lives, and were constantly reminded of death, and the painful toll of work. They worked hard, and their work MEANT something to them.

But today you are just an asset in someone`s company which you really don`t care about. WHAT DO YOU BELIEVE IN? You will DIE one day! I always say you must LIVE for something worth DYING for! Something that is YOU!

Seeing our modern technological achievements with a PERFECT world without death being POSSIBLE, the only philosophically valid purpose, ideology, or life-ambition is working for a perfect-world-uto-pia. KNOWING where technology is heading: This is the only life worth living for. From now on I will proudly present myself as an eternal citizen of the eternal dream.

I am the whole world united, the FFF, and since this is the ultimate utopia, my dream and I am ETERNAL.

Anything as long as we dethrone the Black Order Illuminati!

The problems with the political systems in Norway is the Sabbatean-Frankist-Jesuit-Illuminati. Uproot the cause of world problems, and things return to harmony by itself.

Aside from the Sabbatean-Frankist-Jesuit-Illuminati: We have the best political system in the world, with great diversity, freedom of opinion etc.

Gathering protestors, funding political campaigns, and arranging po-litical concerts/arrangements from the RED-GREEN-CENTER politi-cal Norway should be EASY if we follow up on the Plan.

Most important is that the (entire) 1 State 2 Secret Societies, and 3 Monarchies must fall. And it WILL happen! GLORIOUS!

What power could accomplish this? What forces of rebellion are ac-tive in Norway, and the west today? What can we use, and how can we infiltrate society and win??? What can bring down the state???

1 Angry nationalists losing their nation, borders, rights, culture, welfare, economy, history, truths, culture, religion, language and politicians.

A national-romantic Viking-pagan or Christian opinion.

What is a nation without a nationality? What is a country without borders if not a slave-state of a larger empire? What is a people without a language??? We see ghettos appearing in all major cities, where none speak Norwegian. Is this Norway??? Are we ONE nation? Are we ONE people? Does it matter that we have borders?

Not anymore…

2 A New-Age movement of alternative science, new technology, love and light, and conspiracy theorists. I`d like to unite 1 and 2…

And last, but not least…

Islam?

Yes. Because most Muslims are MUCH more informed, AND angry at the American Jewish Sabbatean-Frankist-Jesuit-Illuminati than the regular Norwegian TV-slave. Because most Muslims know the Jews control world finance, as do all white nationalists. Muslims HATE the Satanic Illuminati, AND the Satanic Jews because of their false-flag war on terror. (For better or worse – I have nothing against the regular Jew.)

This could off-course be utilized to create a world where the cabal loose. Most Muslims are nice, unlike the right-out-blatant SATANISTS that currently rule.

Although this WOULD be better than the current system where millions die of cancer, if we could *use Islam to create the abovementioned conspiracy-reality revolution of science, and better welfare.*

Muslims often rebel, as do Arabs in general, as many good Muslims are non-compromise to evil, which is very unique, and could be used to great effect, unlike Christians who has never done anything against the Jewish-Satanic Illuminati, other than through Martin Luther. God is obviously angry at them.

Ask yourself this: What is a Christian Protestant if he/she does not protest like a protestant??? Huh???

I think Islam might work, but then again: Are they the real religion? And what`s more important: Freedom of speech or technology? Will we be able to criticize Islam and will gays be stoned like some stone-age nightmare???

And what purpose is there in revolution if the new rulers are just as bad as the old? What`s the better evil? If the Satanic Illuminati falls, we save Norwegian national culture, and have advanced medical care and technology for everyone, but loose free speech: What is the purpose of revolution?

We must not repeat the Russian Revolution when the Tsar regime was overthrown by totalitarian communism, of which the 7 of the 12 original revolutionaries in the communist party were Jewish...

If so: We play right into the hands of the Satanic Illuminati, whose primary joy is to bind the human spirit of love, bind the human potential, and bind human evolution. What if a Muslim takeover results in a cold, individualistic society where Christians dare not speak in fear of the Islamic elite.

I thus believe in 1 and 2. Angry nationalists and hippies, although we are inter-religious humanists, and all are welcome to join. Especially angry Muslims who were nuked in their home-countries and had to flee because the Illuminati Jewmerrica warmachine ruined their lives.

You`re welcome…

The battle-plan goes like this:

1. Families of light, love and laughter.

   The secret part of the plan. Gathering all knowledge about all topics, and recruiting members for unofficial private-school cell-groups of love and light, to prepare movies, writing books, making posters, flyers, planning concerts, planning protests, planning love, light, and laughter parades, as well as fashion, and slogans (like love and light) will be important. Infiltrate and recruit a network of revolutionaries from all sectors of society including politicians, doctors, lawyers and policemen. Prepare all groundwork underneath the radar of all media already in stage 1.

2. The disclosure.

   The day we go public. Starting a meme-war, and Facebook groups will be essential, but we must be careful not to mix religion, or ethnic hate into the picture, because that`s when t.h.e.y can shut you down. We must go along whatever political flow in the nation to our advantage.

   You must be very dedicated to victory, and start professional, larger media-organizations with newspapers, and educational centres with classes/lectures with for instance pdf presentations. It won`t do with simple claims like I do in this book. You need FACTS, and EDUCATED people from stage 1.

And if you don't prepare all this in stage 1, they will easily shut you down in stage 2, before you can really begin... Make it so that people will HAVE to see that supporting the People's Army is the right thing...

Involve ourselves in politics REVEALING ourselves as the People's Army, (sort of like a Joker version of the Anonymous movement.) Why so serious when they (state, power-brokers, money-brokers) don't care about your health, your soul, your culture or your race???

Our most important objective in this phase will be getting People's Army's investigative journalists to make interviews with politicians, philantropists, royals, elite, and scientists where they are confronted with the evidence of their crimes, for instance the cures to cancer, which they will have to admit exists, afterwhich we work hard on creating these documentaries for public disclosure. This will be our first priority and should set an example for the rest of the world.

3. The awakening.

Our work in the media is a success, people are waking up, and the People's Army rebel, and crave a reformation of science, physics, history, education, and medicine due to the previous hardcore exposure of conspiracy reality.

The people then go to the streets CRAVING the best available technology and medicine! This is where we beging focusing on a school curriculum reform, because this will awaken future generations, and be a revolution they can't put out. You must think 100 years ahead, just like they do...

The most important part of the Revolution is education of children through gathering our scientist members to re-write school-books which must be handed out after they were created in phase 1.

Phase 3 will be initiated when we have enough funding, only so we can get MORE funding for creating our own futuristic People's Army youth camps, and eventually villages with water-powered cars, water-powered hydroplants, and private schools, being <u>active in media</u>, uniting with Michael Tellinger's Ubuntu and Sasha Stone's NewEarthNation, putting MASSIVE stress on the mainstream media and mainstream science and politicians to where our idea either spreads, or they seize us as criminals.

They can kill a single scientist, easily. But how can they kill five people if all drive water-powered cars, and post it online? How can they attack us when we're making fun of them in a way that the lay-man will understand???

Build cars not only to drive them, but to drive the people furious!!! And how about Tesla's flying car??? And anti-gravity propulsion? I know several who would build them, but lack the great funding, engineers and materials.

4.   The Coup d'état.

When we have our own private schools, our village, our media-channels, have a firm foothold in every political party, and a great percentage of the population is in support of our political party and independent courts of justice, the evidence that the state is ruled by a foreign monetary crime syndicate will be so obvious.

That is when the FFF get together all political parties, noble houses both foreign and domestic, organizations of interest, write our own public constitution of independence, preferably crown a new King, create a never-ending carnival of love, light, lust and laughter enlightenment campaign in front of the media and parliament, and storm them when the police lower their guns, as they have nothing to loose, before we broadcast the long-prepared disclosures for three hours straight on all national TV, and announce the world`s first Illuminati Free Nation, with utopian promises to the rest of the world, with the people`s court declaring that any support of the conspiracy of the previous regime IS treason to both old and new constitutions, humanity, international law, and national law.

5. Or a transition to the FFF through majority of votes.

Our revolution should end with a coup-d`etat with the cabal taken into custody by the People`s Court of the People`s Army, surrendering, and admitting to their COUNTLESS crimes in court on public television, that they lied to us about Utøya 22/7, deceived us in the war on terror, etc.

But the best would be to win the election, something like: Getting the people to announce their new King themselves, use the king to throw out, and criminalize all corruption (freemasons, intelligence-agencies) as the King is the head of the freemasonic lodge, an essential takeover we must plan.

For stage 5 to work, we simply need to advance with public opinion in any major political party, be it FRP, SV or Arbeiderpartiet, etc, and we need a great super-star scientist dictator messiah-figure. A left-wing party would be the easiest in most nations…

But we would have to infiltrate the parties, so to do that, we need to start with reforming science, schoolbooks, and history, in part 1, so that the younger generation will be incorruptible with non-compromise to Satanism of the PST, the Freemasons, and the OTO lodges that rule all the west, by destroying Newtonian, Darwinian, and Quantum Physics, educating children on chemtrails, morgellons, and the monetary crimes of the American NWO.

We must make all banks into one national-state-bank, fix the economy, drain the swamp, and build up infrastructure. We will give the people technology of a Golden Age, and destroy the elite technocracy monopoly on money, history, science, knowledge, health and medicine.

As of today, all nations in the world take interest-loans from private banks (the Rothschild conglomerate) so that the government pay interest! The magnitude of people, and the secrecy this involves is no less than the chemtrail conspiracy! And all potential enemies are bought with sex and violence. God forbid.

Then we could use our now NATIONALIZED OIL-FUND to build a strong currency and inland economy: Norway would become the strongest currency in 4-5 years. Easily.

All history books will be re-written, as will all school-books, and books in universities, with permanent ban on the worst quackademia.

All in all: Our MAIN focus is <u>investigative journalism</u>, a media organization of alternative science, alternative medicine, and conspiracy realities, with the aim of inciting people to action, combined with a self-sufficient society (preferably village like the Tesla village we have in Croatia) where we can apply these people to work, in addition to a private school/educational centre. That should do it for the secret onlyresultscount (ORC) group I`m involved in.

Our future schoolbooks will never forget the NWO criminals!

Remember this. Your worldview reality is built on fictional lies. Destroy the world of lies. Conspiracy IS reality. Not conspiracy THEORY! Conspiracy RESEARCH!

Conspiracy-REALITY! CRIMINAL reality…

WE the PEOPLE decide reality: And the rebel movement, although scattered, have written books, the science - the proof of their conspiracy. MILLIONS of books. The PA will GET these books.

The people must REMEMBER their historical ENEMY through ALL HISTORY!!!

The HIDEOUS criminal, Satanic Illuminati that we OUTLAWED are BACK!!! NOOOO!!! We defeated them once before, and now we will CRUSH them for their sins.

When we win: All will know their CRIMES during the last 2 centuries from schoolbooks. The world will HATE the Satanic Illuminati and fear evil SOO much they can NEVER rise again, EVER, in ANY future. Because of the SCOPE, and GRAVITY of their crime! Is that not a FANTASTIC thought!?! A hope to LIVE for??? To defend your nations?!?

YOU can make that happen! Don`t forget to DREAM!!! You can create a FREE world of water-powered cars, FLYING cars, free energy, and medical technology so you will certainly NEVER DIE! That IS reality! Wow!

Just imagine FLYING into the hidden valleys of the Norwegian woods and saying hi to all of the little elves!

When YOU, and YOUR political party of the People`s Army WIN, and YOU create the First Free Federation, every man will get a minimum salary (social support) because robots will do most of the work, and the technology has made short process of all disease, and transformed the regular citizen into a superman!!! Mankind will be united, and happy forever, able to focus on ENJOYING life!!!

A world without poverty, disease, famine or even DEATH! Why will this Free New Socialist World be global, peaceful and united? Because the People`s Army defeated  mankind`s enemy: The Satanic Illuminati. THAT will be enough to unite ALL religions, and ALL ethnicities for ALL eternity, because we the people will never forget our schoolbooks… We defeated the mafia. The corporationalists, the super-rich, and the technocracy.

When children learn we defeated evil, secrecy, and conspiracy at school, it will never rise again! Just like Nazi Germany can never rise again!

Don`t you understand??? I envision a glorious People`s Army victory in Norway that goes global, UNITES ALL HUMANITY in dethroning the evil conglomerate!!! Together we will sit upon their carcass for as long as anything CAN last…

The world will be ONE, WON, and FOREVER UNITED through the inter-religious ethics of the humanistic religion of Source, Love and Light, which ALL can agree upon! Read my book on the subject.

Someone wants me dead. But THEY shall lose THEIR head, whence we have the people and proof. MY head MUST remain on my shoulders where it belongs. Or else: The world faces a major loss which might be the fatal blow to all humanity.

Repetition of what solutions we discovered.

Is to awaken the masses, and accomplish disclosure of secret technology, knowledge, medicine etc. We must do our job in media. *School curriculums must be rewritten. An alliance of alternative scientists must be formed in an anarchistic TESLA village in the beautiful valleys of Norway.* There is one such Tesla village in Croatia, and one in Mauritius… I had the opportunity to settle there, along with Tomislav Tesla, and Harry Rhodes, my dear friend, but had to pass…

There we will have our enlightened private-schools, free electricity, and media broadcast. If we have ONE true, enlightened, perfectibilist society: We have won, because one light is lit, one light is enough to expel all darkness in a room.

All worldwide darkness will fade, because everyone will want our schools, true education, our technology, our solutions to all world problems, and our philosophy of source, love and light…

This has been my dream since I was as young as I can remember. I would fly into future timelines in lucid dreams, and see all these AMAZING villages with pyramids, elves, beautiful carvings, flying cars – etc – faaar into the future! And what better place to start one than beautiful Norway which is FULL of hidden, beautiful valleys, *only accessible through antigravity/levity propulsion transport.* I remember I dreamt of BEAUTIFUL gardens, and survivalist farms deep in hidden valleys like "operation Rivendell." Lol.

My life`s ambition has always remained the same: Cultivating soil, and soul in perfect symbiosis with nature in the beautiful landscape of rugged Norway: Now perfect for settlement once we reach antigravity/levity propulsion.

ARE YOU WITH ME?

Ask yourself. As *all* history, philosophy, science, and law undergoes the scientific method of the 21st century: How come *all* religion is allowed to exist while not undergoing the scientific method, and validating itself???

Think about that for a second, or read it again…

After all the people it`s killed!

God is not a hypothesis anymore if you can PROVE him. Magick is not magical anymore when you know of the ether. The SOURCE-FIELD. It becomes reduced to science.

Ask yourself this: If God is real, and science is reality; How come science doesn't prove God? Because it DOES prove God!!! That's why they don't teach you SOURCE-FIELD physics at school!!! Because FREEMASONS made the educational system to be about "survival of the fittest" as is their Luciferian agenda! It's a death-cult about murder and betrayal! Not the love of the source-field and human nature!

When politics, and law is mixed with religion, we have a problem. Especially sharia.

After the secret People's Army have secretly united scientists, liberals, hippies, anarchists, humanists, journalists, lawyers, whistleblowers, etc, from all levels of society, and institutions under our humanistic common banner of FFF, we will prosecute the Satanic Illuminati, AND their religious institutions in our own courts, once we have our own Illuminati free nation, reed out the poisonous virus that has infected the Church, the Mosques, the Synagogues, all Abrahamism in general, and it's people.

It should not be too hard to take back power to the people. The Satanic Illuminati cancer has infiltrated our economy, culture, media, government, education, hospitals, intelligence agenises, police, and courts.

It's all corrupt, so it's very simple. Just leave it and start from the beginning. Give up on the Old World. Leave Babylon and build a Free New World. Build a garden in your backyard. Start today! Start a family of light! Be a survivalist anarchist! Join the People's Army! Join me and make my words your own!

They ruin our lands from within to make us their future slaves... They have become so big they can no longer hide and will be easy to expose whence we are united as a People's Army. Once we are OUTSIDE the system, and gaze on it from within our village with our media-organization, and investigative journalists: How can you NOT notice the Satanic Illuminati? The stinking elephant that lies to everyone in the room??? And EVERYBODY knows that politicians lie.

They became rulers of the world through evil. How much more potent is love? Why shouldn`t YOU be prime minister??? Most people I meet on the street have much better answers to politics than ANY politician…

They started simple with a conspiracy just like us! The Illuminati started as anarchistic etheric scientists and teachers. Although we start to revert all of their quackedemia lies and their monetary conglomerate. They became corrupted by knowledge, technology, monetary power, wealth, sex, and the urge to destroy to please Satan… How much more will we not succeed through love, light, lust and laughter???

All we need to do is conspire and organize in secret just like THEY did! Organize Anonymous, and the FFF`s People`s Army in secret AGAINST the Satanic Illuminati, infiltrate, and take BACK your economy, media, government, and re-create our laws, and lands from OUTSIDE the system: In a village somewhere.

When you stand on top of the mountain like Zarathustra, and get the bird perspective like from an airplane: How often do you not come to conclusions through new perspectives??? That IS the way to freedom, and believe me, you will cry a lot, as I have…

If you see the world history from the top of a mountain outside the system, it is easy to notice that the Satanic Illuminati declared a war on ¨we the people¨ a long time ago, probably with the Annunaki priesthood in early Sumer… It`s serious… If I were to define the rulers of the current system from ancient times up til today, I would define them as ¨ANTI-HUMAN ACTIVISTS. ¨ Nothing else. ALL they sell are lies meant to destroy us! Even our very food, and the air we BREATHE!

They are pushing every form of oppression possible, trying to destroy as much as possible, in the shortest time possible… That is the definition of the rich-Satanic (Rothschild), and royal elite ruling the multinational corporationalists (like George Soros) , the technocratic intelligence agenises, and their bought politicians.

BLOODY SATANISTS!

There will be no bloodshed, just a massive awakening, and a peaceful transition back to normality, where the government, and monarch will be forced to abdicate, followed by public tv-broadcast of their lawsuit, and a public disclosure on technology. We must gain control over the national media at ANY cost.

David Icke, and David Wilcock has done quite well, not that I support them...

NOW it's YOUR turn! And IF we gain little political ground and come only half ways: We will create the public court and trial these criminals ANYWAYS: Present or not. Crime is crime. Law is law. Life is life. Death is death.

Remember: Our main goal is to teach children. Teachings in these families of Light. Teaching them knowledge, and the crimes of the Satanic Illuminati so it's victims are remembered, and so the Satanic Illuminati never rise again.

Knowledge is power! Media is power! Power to the People!

Our first target as I've already said, is getting investigative disclosure of cancer cures to the mainstream media, because they are privately owned, because when many see "hey, they're anti-human activists!", they often wake up to the rest of the picture.

From now on, you should be really angry if the media does not only report facts, breakthroughs in science, healing, humanist work, human progress, and have a single goal: Uniting all to create utopia for all. No more celebrity-slander, fearmongering, apathic programming, wars, and rubbish in the media!

When we control the media, the public outcry for disclosure, and justice will be too large. The only thing that stops the Army of the People when we have media is... Nothing... Dethroning the King, the government, the police, and even the lodges will be too easy...

All too easy.

All we need is to make the media serve the people again, not the Rothschild conglomerate who owns them.

I can`t WAIT until the day of disclosure! People will be SO angry, realizing they`ve been lied to, and that they`ve had it. No more monopoly over the people! From now on, the PEOPLE should control the media!

Plain truth, citizen anger, and constant protests against the media will lower their morale. When the police lower their guns to our charade, as they have nothing to loose, the Love Light Laughter parade will march into the media, and demand a nationwide public broadcast on the Satanic Illuminati system, hidden technology, and their HIDEOUS crimes.

You will make videos and make them fast. This protest alone should lead to global breakdown of the system, and they know it.

With 21st century media being everywhere in our daily lives, media has become the world`s number 1 system of governance. If you control what people see, hear, and thus control their automatic response, and ability reason: You basically have complete OWNERSHIP over their thoughts, and thus their minds, and thus their very SOULS…

The MEDIA is an EVIL fear-installing PROPAGANDA-MACHINE! And Einsteinian masonic rubbish of Nasa`s blue marble is worse than any propaganda in Nazi-Germany!

The Freemasonic lodge was OUTLAWED in all Nazi-Germany occupied territory!

At some point: Lawyers, *schoolteachers*, scientist, doctors, and private hospitals will start joining us. Teachers, parents and scientists will start presenting an alternative reality to what you`ve been told at school.

Join us! Away with gullible apathy! You are DIRECTLY responsible for your children, right? What world do we leave them???

Prepare for a reality of sacred geometry, and perfect intelligent design.

Be ready to embrace a world where mankind is holy, science proves God, and holy mother nature has every cure.

If nature has a problem: Nature has a way to fix it. God/Source-field made it that way. <3

When we have ONE independent state of the First Free Federation, the Satanic Illuminati will never rise again. They will be so HATED for their crimes that *they will never be forgotten from history-books.*

That`s the vision I fight for. So should you. Free children in a futuristic, free and perfect school of truth, real science, love, honesty and care.

Ending words and the point of this book.

I will end by saying revolution is the only solution. Why? For no other goal than utopia is worth living for.

Create the idea of a society so good - a golden age of religious, humanistic, and technological breakthroughs SO great it will set the template for ALL the world to infinity…

Gain the knowledge and create an idea so good that it`s very inception would make its completion inevitable. Today I created this idea, and it should not be too hard to complete as a group conscience, or a people.

That`s why they install fear, wars, resulting with immigration, thus creating an individualist society of survival of the fittest. Cultural Marxism preparing for economic Marxism: The New World Order.

But I believe that when one is awake, it will spread to the others like ripples in the ether. And hey! I`m awake!

Therefore YOU`re now awake.

As I already said, there is much more at stake than opinion, race, politics and religion. We need something to unite all the people! This isn`t about race. Our future, and health is at risk.

Ok. Let`s get to the point of this book… I have friends, and family who have died of cancer…, as do you…

My uncle for instance… He was a GREAT Christian, and I never had the opportunity to know him, as he died from cancer very young.

IF we don`t reach mass-awareness, and disclosure of technology, and conspiracy reality to cure cancer in a free country today, *millions, potentially BILLIONS more will die prematurely to fill the pockets and Agenda 21 goals of the UN`s pharmaceutical companies.* That is the point of this book. World population growth has halted globally, with only a few countries in Africa sadly growing in population.
8 billion is more than enough, but all the west, all the East (including Bangladesh) , and the rest of the world get about 2-3 children on average.
Keep peace in the world for as long as possible, avert war at all cost, and everything will revert back to harmony by the goodness of human nature.

And if you don`t act today, then how will you act in a future police state where government controls the internet, and have strict monopoly on scientific facts? But they need more war for that to happen, just like they took your rights of free-speech, and survey you after they instigated civil war through 9/11, false flag attacks, leading to war and demographic crisis dividing the nation.

They need a WW3, and we must act before they start it, and impeach all our freedoms in the name of ¨peace and security¨, reducing us to slaves. The government is censoring more, and more knowledge, and serve sex, money and power. (Rothschild).
That`s what at stake… The freedom of all humanity…

This is not a one nation revolution about race or religion. This is a global revolution about taking back the power to the people. It`s about knowledge and taking back media. The First Free Federation. The first Illuminati free space on human soil! Where truth is truth, and quackademia is no more.

For media is knowledge, and knowledge is power: Power to the people!

I want a humanistic revolution about laughter, love and light/enlightenment...
But Thomas, why should this be a socialist revolution, and not a blue, or right-wing revolution (of choir-boy suitcases)???
It should and could be, at least in the west. Read my Kingdom of God, but because there has never been a right-wing revolution, and the media installs fear of them, because the left is the new political-economic establishment, and because of sick inside-jobs like Utøya, it is time to use the political zeitgeist current, plagiarize the left and make it anti-super-rich-establishment again! For now... We also need a Daenerys.

The idea is to make a left-wing-party represent a future welfare system of medical treatment that is so cheap, and good, it should be global by 2050!!!
IF, and WHEN we succeed; technology is used FOR the people, and not AGAINST them!!!
We will have such advancements in healthcare, industry, and labour compared to other nations, that our economy will boost exponentially! Free healthcare will be so cheap with our new technology that *we will all become socialists in the future.*
Although this is not what I would have wanted, it is our best and (perhaps) last chance of making the current mad-world a little better...
Instead of today`s suffering, the people of the future will be happy, tolerant, and enlightened. Most will be able to focus on enjoying life rather than labouring.

With all illness gone, and advancement in robotics, a smaller percentage will have jobs, and the rest must be cared for through citizen salary – social welfare from the government, and thus we are socialists. (I am not, I am an economic-liberalist/capitalist, like the Norwegian party Liberalistene, which is much closer to working Anarchy, but hey, I bet on all horses.)
There will be a sense of social unity, because WE THE PEOPLE screamed out against oppression and won.

Appendix 1. Response to criticism of racism. I am not a racist. Nationalism is only a medium to change the NWO.

I have never been called a racist, but I add this article if so should happen. I am not a racist. In fact, most of my friends have always been immigrants. I didn`t like Norwegians, because they lacked identity, identity which I personally had as a Christian. All other ethnicities had great cultural pride other than Nordics, which is ironic, as the Nordics have are the most different and diverse ethnicity among all the world`s ethnicities, and since Norway was never part of the crimes of WW2.

Nationalism is healthy and has nothing to do with Nazism, but with national-romance, love, integration, and patriotism against general evil, against the New World Order, against conspiracy-theories, against global communist dictatorship, if nationalism is done correctly: Being used to wake the Scandinavians to fight the battle for all humanity, just like the nationalistic Sami, Hawaiian Polynesians, Israelites, or Middle-Eastern citizens fight against the same bloody elephant in the room: The Illuminati`s NWO.

Some Norwegian nationalists point at the mouth of the elephant and say "cultural Marxism!" Some Jihadi fighters point at the feet and say "big-capitalist Rothschild war-broking!" Some American conspiracy theorists point at it`s ass and say "big pharma, Mc-Donalds, CIA false flag terror and chemtrails!" *We see the same big elephant, but we won`t be able to defeat it unless we see each other and unite.*

I myself am pro anything that is non-compromise that expose the lies of the current system, be it communism, ultra-liberalistic anarchism or right-wing nationalism. As long as it exposes their monetary crimes against cancer patients.

Humanity must wake up. It`s not me vs you or him vs her. It`s us vs Illuminati Satanism. A battle against what could only be described as "anti-human activists." Satanism and Illuminati in world-leading positions across the 1. Monetary elite, 2. Technocratic elite, 3. Cultural elite, governmental elite, etc, although the list goes on into further degrees and categories...

We are not fighting an armed conflict but an INFOwar of a revolution renaissance to enlighten the people with cures to cancer, stopping chemtrails, exposing the 9/11 inside job, etc. This isn`t about ideological differences, but about having the opportunity to live long healthy lives, caring for our planet, and getting rid of an ideology, that of Illuminati Satanism, which inhibits all human growth in all diverse nations... To Norway, nationalism might be medium to fight the elephant, while to an Iraqi citizen who lost his family, Jihad might be the medium to fight the same fucking elephant: The Illuminati Rothschild war-banking empire, and Rothschild globalism, as David Icke puts it.

It`s not negative that the world is one, or that it`s one for the first time because of the internet. The problem is chemotherapy, chemtrails, depopulation, wars, and the abovementioned Illuminati leaders of this New World Order. A global world based upon humanistic values is a brilliant idea! Going to war with Afghanistan, Iraq, Lebanon, Syria and Iran is however a (very) bad idea if we want dialogue, and a stable natural growth towards a humanistic future world utopia. The world of human nature is already united through the internet. The world of banking-empires does however have a few wars left. The problem isn`t globalization, but the ones who would be it`s leaders.

Furthermore, if we are to be really scriptural about it, and go against the Jews: Multiculturalism through mass immigration is forbidden by the tower of Babel story in all Abrahamic religions and by common sense. The only reason Rothschild cause wars leading to immigration is to continue being in power. If there was peace, brotherly love and true healthcare, we would not need their hospitals, armies, governments or police. *But if they can create a cold future society of Muslim vs Jew and Christian, LGBT Marxist globalist vs nationalist, and atheist vs religious, with no common world ethic, they will continue being in power because we won`t have the unity to overthrow their monetary system.* The coldness through the diversity of Europe`s future society will crave a strong police-state, and a strong communist government ¨for your own protection"! While it`s nothing more than Satanic population control by elite anti-human activist megalomaniacs.

I want to sell the idea that God has chosen the Nordic people, because *he has*. EVERYONE is chosen to fight along God against the NWO, but the Nordics seem to have missed this, and abandoned their national identity, replaced by Americanisation, political relativism, materialism, post-modernism and out-right-Satanism.
God WANTS them to believe they have a special role in the fight against the Beast NWO, because Nordics are the future minority who lost their country, just like the Jews once lost theirs. The mantle of civilization is passed from one race to another, because the former lost their humanism to materialism...
God also wants to redefine how Nordics view themselves and give them the pride that they lack. Even Africans have more pride than the average Nordic! And that`s a good thing, because pride doesn`t mean we chop each-others heads off. Pride just means we aren`t brainwashed.
Ethnic pride is a natural human thing, just ask any ethnic child. Ethnic pride contributes to world diversity, and Olympic games, sports, independence-day-parades, and meeting other ethnicities as a pub, are friendly examples that ethnic pride is positive, and has nothing to do with war in a time that we all have resources like food and shelter. With food, water, healthcare and partying, humanity has no reason to go to war. Wars were never fought because of racial pride, but because of megalomania, and the same old anti-human, Satanic conspiracy. The beasts of the Bible. Yet today we are all subjugated by the same world authority: Jewish racism.

Nazi Germany only used nationalism as a propaganda tool while the war in reality targeted the freemasons, and the Illuminati conspiracy, the Freemasonic lodge being banned from every country they occupied. Just listen to Hitler going on and on about how Rothschild started WW1 for profit and then destroyed Germany`s economy, enraging the entire nation. It is a fact that the entire reason for WW2 was a response to the same economic Rothschild conspiracy that creates all current wars and upheaval in the world today. This is an evident historical fact seen in the conspiracy-theory nature of the

Nazi-Party, Hitler himself, all his advisors, all his speeches, etc. Nazi-Germany was the world's first Illuminati-free nation comprised of the same conspiracy theorists as today. And by liberating themselves from the Jewish Illuminati, Germany became the world's most powerful nation in only 13 years from after having lost WW1. Historically speaking, there is no difference between a member of the historical Nazi party and a modern day conspiracy theorist, aside from racial views, which was only used to kindle the fire. A Nazi is a conspiracy theorists in battle. A warrior for truth and freedom against anti-human activists, any way you see it.

The entire idea behind Nordicism is to replace Norwegians wrongly attributed identity of Satanic materialism with the our rightful purity, strength, honour and holiness. I want (particularly) blondes to view themselves as God sees them: Their blonde hair, white skin, and blue eyes symbolizing the blue Heaven, the sun, the clouds and in general: Holiness. If they so did, they would be very mighty, and a powerful tool against Satan's New World Order. Satan knows this, and has therefore branded blondes as stupid, promiscuous, naiive, submissive, and as "evil Nazis" or even "offspring of fallen angels." If only the latter were true, then perhaps things would change for the better. Lol.

Just kidding, the Bible is clear that all the sons of Noah are blessed. We're all the same on the inside, but God has given gifts to each race, through his immaculate love for diversity. It goes unsaid that the persona called "God" could only be fully expressed in the creation of all ethnicities, represented with Jesus as Adam. God is thus philosophically in my view both white, black, Asian and Hispanic.

I read the Bible, and then I read dark secrets on the internet. The Jews once represented God's fight against Babylon, Egypt, Rome, globalism, multiculturalism, Satanism, *but have become the very thing they once fought against.* I cannot bring myself to believe they are his chosen people! Surely, out of all the people in the world today, God has chosen the naiive, hopeful, loving, peaceful and civilized humanistic Nordic conspiracy theorists in their resistance against the NWO.

They are in the exact same position as Nazi Germany, or the historical Jews when they left Egypt and represent the entire human race, having lost their first Illuminati-free country, being enslaved by Babylon and Egypt, wandering in the Sinai desert searching for the future homeland for all ethnicities of the Earth: The first free federation of likeminded organizations. The world`s first Illuminati-free nation. A nation where God rules, not banking-profit. A nation of futuristic healthcare FOR humanity, not against it. A nation with free electricity as envisioned by Nicola Tesla. *A nation free of the old Satanic conspiracy: Today represented by the Illuminati.*

And while I often address Jews, Jesuits, and Freemasons, I do so only because many of these are involved in the anti-human Illuminati conspiracy, not because I am a racist. My best friends are f.i Jews. The regular Haredi Israelite hates his war-broking Rothschild government as much, if not more than any Norwegian nationalist. It`s the same bloody elephant in the room.
But with the internet, partying, healthcare, food, water and shelter, humanity has no reason to wage war for resources. This is the first time in history… Had it not been for Rothschild trying to stay in power through war-broking, putting us against each-other to create a cold future society in need for their elected pay-dogs on top: A police-state "for your protection".
The Jews have played their part in history and have become a racist, fascist, powerful world empire of conglomerates. And power is prone to abuse.
It is time another chosen people took over, interbred in the same way, and kept their bloodline purity, just like the Jews have for 2000 years. Or else, blonde hair will die out. It makes more sense that kind, peaceful, naive blondes are chosen, and preserve their cultural and racial purity than Jews, whom look like everyone else anyways. Why Jews are allowed to be racist while blondes are not, I wonder… None of Scandinavia was in any way associated with Nazi Germany.

Does it matter? Only if can be used to fight the greater war… I see the world dying. I am afraid not only for the survival of European ethnic culture, but for humanism, the ecology, and all that stands in the way of the Illuminati`s destructive elephant. I am not a racist, and this battle is not about race, but the survival of mankind, which is the purpose for my writings.

One of the first battles (along with the Middle-East) against the future communistic New World Order is being fought in Scandinavia, as Nordics are losing their countries and culture to the demographic crisis, with big-capital-war being the root problem (not the immigrants) , and I think therefore that Nordics should use that anger, not against other ethnic groups, but through conspiracy theory, to wake up, and fight not only for themselves, but for all humanity, in the greater war against this monetary conspiracy of war-broking.

Perhaps the Nordics and Arabs should unite, as the army under Daenerys Targaryen, to overthrow the moneylenders, the usury and whore-bribery of the big-capital Lannister war-machine of anti-human-activists???

I personally could not give a damn about race; if people go to Hell! It is the greater war that matters, as we put aside all differences (for now), and unite in the infowar to wake up and unite all mankind to the conspiracy of the New World Order.

What worth does nationalism have to me as a Christian who believe all races are equal and saved??? Nationalism is only a response that wakes people up to the GREATER conspiracies.

As Norway is hijacked by an Illuminati pirate-ship destroying her people, human rights, culture and economy, you might say that Scandinavians are CHOSEN, as they are the prime example of the war against the NWO in the world today, so that it is God`s will to pour out his zeal, passion, love, strength and courage over Nordics, to take back their country from the Illuminati, because the war of the world is being fought in Scandinavia.

Why is the war of the world being fought in Scandinavia? Because, if Norway actually exposed the lies of Illuminati government, through inherent nationalism waking them up, and if Norway became the world`s first Illuminati free nation, which they are the best candidate for as they have the wrath, the riches, the oil, the wits and the resources, they would represent a light of free healthcare, electricity, and MAJOR scientific breakthroughs to the entire world; the turning of the tides for the globalist Illuminati war against humanity, as the

Illuminati would lose their first and most important battle to destroy humanism and Christianity.

Look at diversity in nature. Human plurality is the common sense of nature philosophy, history, state-science and religion. Biblically forbidden in all Abrahamic religions through the Tower of Babel story. God meant for diversity.

Take for instance the ecology in China. Is it the same as in Norway? Should we force Chinese ecology to Norway because it is plant-racism??? Diversity is natural and beautiful. Diversity is not multiculturalism through a mixture of demographics, but through unity of nations, not through the EU, but through common human ethics in independent nation states. The humanist ethics of the Greco-Roman-Judeo-Christian values that the entire west is built upon. Peace cannot come through a mixture of ethnics, but through a unity of ethics. And my candidate is Christianity.
Aside from that, I wish I could do more for the *greater good*. This book is such an effort. Thank you. I want a better world for everyone.

Appendix 2. Here is a repetition of our plan.

1. The study and secret recruitment phase/families of love and light. Unite in families, secret schools, and study-groups of love and light (love=morale and light=enlightenment/science). Cooperate to discover all conspiracies, secrets, truths, and technologies hidden.

Hoard books, make movies, write books on this until your knowledge-basis of all scientific fields is UTTERLY complete to the point where the pyramid WILL tumble. Knowledge is power. Power to the PEOPLE! *This is the secret stage.* You spread in cells, and recruit members in all sectors of society. Infiltrate, and recruit people in the political left (and right). Recruit all members secretly through letters, and usb-pens. Avoid any media exposure. Recruit internationally and gather everyone to focus solely on reforming ONE nation because when one light is lit, everyone will want it.

2. The media phase. Start everything you can from facebook-groups, meme-wars to media-organizations, newspapers, etc, to spread all the knowledge of truth you have gained to the people. *You must secretly promote interest in hidden knowledge, hidden history, hidden science (like etheric physics), and start private schools built upon this new physics and reality.* Focus on the root causes and most obvious elephants only, things that will really get the attention of our primary target: Children, youths, liberals, leftists, hippies, bikers, anarchists, new-agers, Muslims, nationalists, and all who believe in conspiracy reality.

3. The awakening. The movement has gained media attention, and the people are waking up. Push harder. Start pushing your agenda into left-wing politics, mainstream media, organize public humiliating *laughter protests, Love, Light, Lust and Laughter parades* and concerts: To get the people to fight for their RIGHTS of having truth, and the best available medicine and technology. Peel the serious face of the politicians until they`re naked liars and laugh at them. You will win.

4 The Revolution. Parade with the crave of a media disclosure, and government step-down to the FFF`s PA, and start reformation in the sciences of economics, physics, history, medicine etc. Build up inland economy, start science-facilities, villages, private-schools, think tanks, and welfare organizations etc. Be a light to the world.

I have no other goal than victoriously singing, dancing, and parading the streets with an army of love, light and laughter. We will avoid all stigma by being joyous, humorous and life filled. Not stereotypes the media can blackwash like bald-head Nazis. I mean… Come on… Did you hear you lost the war??? It means Hitler ain`t gonna save you this time.

Now we can celebrate for all eternity, and hand over work to robots. Not really. Working is good. But anyways…

Here is how it might happen. The Army of the People enlightens the FURIOUS cancer patients, and their relatives (which includes all humanity – rich and poor, left and right). They put on their yellow vests, and protest with our documentaries, books, and knowledge until every marionette, and police realize they serve a tyranny of terrorists, and surrender to the people.

What`s left standing is the Satanic cabal of secret societies, and their governments of career politicians. Naked liars shaking in their boots from our laughter. Every citizen protest, and denounces the government, police, and refuse to vote for them, wanting the revolution and perhaps a new King???

Yes… ONE good-old-traditional way to consider, is the old Alpha-Male Civilizer Sun-King Horus. They won`t be able to shut THAT down, because nothing encourages people with pitchforks more than a super-idol King. (Which is basically what a King was back in the days, before the Hannovers took over, anyways.)

This might be a better route than going through the political arena, because *you simply cannot deny the people the right for a King.* And what`s even better is that *all the King dictates is law and secret societies.* So, the pyramid will fall brick by brick whatever happens, IF you follow our commands, and raise up Messiahs.

I have given you a jump start! From here on starts your journey into conspiracy-REALITY!

Say what???

What is a secret Bilderberg meeting if not conspiracy???

Do you have any better term for it? The Bilderberg Group was formed by people who openly profess alliance to the New World Order as late Pr. George Henry Walker Bush, and Henry Kissinger!!!

Wake up and put a smile on that face. ;)

Laughter, Love and Light will win against all odds, if you do what is written in this book. 100% guaranteed!

So.........................

Feel free to join humanity. Feel free to join the First Free Federation`s Army of the People.

Nobody owns an idea, and nobody owns the People`s Army, which currently does not exist. I would also like to point out that I`m a pacifist, and that we fight an info-war. Never have I incited towards violence in any of my books.

I encourage you to make this book, these words, and this dream into *your own* dream.

If you liked this book, read my other book on revolution:

The Kingdom of God!

Or read my scientific, inter-religious Law of All Golden Ages:

The Wisdom of all Golden Ages, and The metaphysical Law of Source, Love and Light.

The re-discovered Eternal Law of All Creation! A law that unites science, metaphysics, philosophy and religion for the first time in modern history!

I believe it`s humanism can really knit this world together.

Thomas Eidsaa. Stay tuned and create paradise utopia!